POPULATION AND AGRICULTURAL DEVELOPMENT: SELECTED RELATIONSHIPS AND POSSIBLE PLANNING USES

Development Research and Training Service, Policy Analysis Division.

Food and Agriculture Organization of the United Nations.

Rome, December 1977

M-04

ISBN 92-5-100490-0

PREFACE

Growing concern about rapid population growth in the developing countries has been reflected in recent years in the search for effective policies to curb it.   The traditional attitude of economists to bypass the population aspects has led to neglect of the study of interrelationships between population trends and development patterns.   The resulting gaps in our knowledge have tended to weaken the conceptual basis for the design of any meaningful population policy.   The UN World Population Conference (1974) recognized this, while recommending that governments should develop national policies and programmes relating to the growth and distribution of their populations.   The Conference accordingly recommended, among other things, that research efforts should be intensified to develop knowledge of social, economic and political interrelationships with population trends.

This has given further impetus to efforts to discover the manner in which demographic and socio-economic variables inter-act, in the hope of finding a practical way of making development planning more demography-responsive.   Some progress has already been achieved in developing, and disseminating to the planners, analytical tools appropriate for formulating and evaluating development goals and policies taking into account the effects of a changing demographic situation.   However, much more work needs to be done to analyse the reverse relationship, with a view to obtaining insights on appropriate socio-economic policies that can influence demographic trends in a desirable direction.   The present volume marks only a partial attempt in this direction.

The modest objective of this report is to help those concerned in planning for agricultural development gain an understanding of selected aspects of the population-development relationships that may be relevant to their work.   It is in line not only with FAO's general interest in this area of policy analysis, but also with its concern for helping in the acceleration of the pace of agricultural and rural development.   In fact, agriculture is almost at the centre of the population-development scene, because of its dominating position in the economic structure and demographic processes of the developing countries.   A large part of the increment in total population in these countries takes place in a socio-economic environment woven around agriculture and the economic activities associated with it.   In this situation, agriculture is in a constant state of challenge, to meet the expanding claims on it and, in particular, to satisfy the food needs of a growing population.   Further compounding the challenge are the increasingly grave problems of rural-urban migration and unemployment, which are, on one side, demography-related phenomena, and on the other, conditioned in a large measure by the pattern of agricultural development.

The report synthesizes a number of contributions by different authors on selected agriculture-specific topics and case studies in the area of population-development relationships.   It addresses itself mainly to agricultural planners and policy makers; and Chapter VI draws some conclusions, specifically keeping in view their possible planning applications. [1]/ The contributions (detailed in Chapter I, and the Appendix), as well as this Report, have been prepared with the financial assistance of the United Nations Fund for Population Activities, under project INT/73/P02, of which this is the final Report. The assistance of UNFPA is gratefully acknowledged.

The different contributions were synthesized into the present Report by Professor Pan A. Yotopoulos of Stanford University, and Dr. N. Alexandratos, Economist in the Policy Analysis Division of FAO, who also had overall coordinating responsibility for the finalization of the different contributions and of this Report.

· J.P. Bhattacharjee
Director
Policy Analysis Division

[1]/ Two companion volumes in the same series /Baldwin 1975; Cairncross 1977/ deal with related subjects.

CONTENTS   PAGE

CONTENTS PAGE

LIST OF TABLES

CHAPTER I

INTRODUCTION

In recent years, population has become an important component in the process of planning, both in general and in agricultural development planning in specific. It is ironic, but probably true, that there might have been no impetus for this novel concern had the historically unprecedented rates of population growth observed in the last few decades not happened to coincide with also unprecedented rates of growth in Gross Domestic Product. While the rates of increase in population need not cause surprise, the inability of growth in GDP to deliver development was unexpected. Within the operative framework of the orthodox economics of development, growth is inconsistent with the persistence of widespread poverty. Even worse, the agricultural sector in less developed countries (LDCs) continued to show stubborn technological backwardness, while the technologically advanced sector displayed a general inability to make a significant contribution to absorbing unemployment. In these circumstances, it was considered axiomatic that the global population explosion was hindering the spread of development within LDCs and widening the economic distance between the rich nations and the third world.

As a minimum, the real case for an active population policy was based on three propositions /Seers 1973 p. 12/. (a) With a fast-growing labour force, it is impossible to relieve unemployment and poverty; (b) growing pressure of population makes it impossible to expand education and other social services; (c) growing population pressure increases the need for foreign aid, thus fostering economic dependency, and postponing the attainment of genuine independence by LDCs. While these propositions are generally accepted, the literature suggests that there has been significant variance in opinion as to whether rapid population growth is an absolute deterrent, or at worst a non-trivial retarder of economic and social development /Berelson 1976/. This divergence of opinion, however, has hardly been reflected in the policy solution which has been emphatically accepted — the dissemination of birth-control information and devices. The fact that birth control technology can be provided at a relatively low price has greatly enhanced its appeal as a policy instrument.

More recent experience throughout the world has led experts to question the population policy approaches which operate exclusively on the demographic side. It has been recognized that families must be provided with the motivation, as well as with the means, to limit births. A significant contribution of the World Population Conference, as well as of the World Food Conference, was the recognition that the basis for an effective solution of population problems was, first and foremost, socio-economic transformation. Development planning, as a result, is in search of population policies which combine the socio-economic side with the demographic side. While this is a laudable objective, two problems must be kept clearly in mind. Although development may induce population control, in many parts of the world the achievement of relatively high levels of living and development may be postponed or even thwarted by heavy population pressures. Second, development is a plausible necessary condition for population control, but it is unlikely to provide a sufficient condition. Not every kind of development is likely to be equally effective in reducing the rates of increase in population.

The proposition that economic development and population growth are interdependent may seem almost self-evidence. Yet, traditionally, the tendency has been to consider either factor within the narrow confines of its own sicentific discipline, treating the other as a constraining factor. As regards development, for example, "For a long time now, economic theory has evolved without much interest in population problems, and some of the difficulties in trying to force them back into economics may be due to this" /Ohlin 1976, p. 14/. More specifically, population has commonly been considered exogenous to the economic system, and so has income to the demographic system. Economics has thus generally been concerned with maximizing common welfare or per capita incomes, given the population level, and demography has been concerned with determining the optimum population size, the one which maximizes per capita income, given the relations of production. Only minor concessions have been made within this framework in consideration of the "other discipline". Demography has introduced the theory of demographic transition, which originally considered the levels of "socio-economic development" as determinants of demographic trends — and which was soon metamorphosed into a special case of the more general theory of social change. Similarly, economics endogenized family fertility decisions in the benefit-cost analysis of children —

and this soon became referenced to social conditioning and to differences in tastes.

The Legacy of Partial Approaches and Future Targets for Research

At this point, two questions of interest arise: (i) What has been the result of these partial approaches to economics and to demography? and (ii) What has been the cause of such watertight treatment of the subject in both fields?

The payoff to making a host of subtle problems external to a field of analysis - by assigning them as charges to a first-cousin discipline - is that one can make unambiguous predictions. These, in relation to population and to betterment of life, have ranged from bust to boom. Malthus, with more respect for arithmetic than for demography or economics, predicted an increasing state of human deprivation as a result of his postulates on food supplies and on population. The Club of Rome /D. H. Meadows et al. 1972, pp. 48-58, 147/, by parametrizing current population growth, present dietary levels and yields at twice the current yield levels, concluded that the world would run out of food supplies by the middle of the next century. And on the other side Revelle /1974, 1975/ estimated that with appropriate technology and sufficient purchased inputs (equivalent to the inputs used for maize production in Iowa), 50 to 60 billion people could be provided with high quality diet, or almost 100 billion people could be fed at a minimum level of subsistence.

Economics carries the burden for success or failure in these two latter exercises. Even worse, the magnitude of the burden is often left unspecified. Pawley /1971/, for example, would have no difficulty in agreeing with Revelle's cornucopia, since he estimates that, by the year 2070, cultivable area could be quadrupled to 6 billion hectares, provided that two major technological breakthroughs occur: first, that humid tropical soils could be fully deforested and cultivated continuously, and, second, that sea water could be desalinized at low enough costs to become available for cultivation. The question which Pawley implies is whether this is likely. In other words, grand, global predictions of this type cannot only be wrong; they are also uninteresting. Societies have built-in brakes and shock absorbers which arrest the speed and cushion the fall. But one would have to search inside the machinery, through a number of intricate parts, to discover those instruments. They cannot be observed by simply looking at the exterior configuration of the social vehicle.

This brings us to the second point relating to the causes of the watertight treatment of population and development. On the side of economics, at least, there is no ambiguity about the motivation for this approach and about the cause of the neglect of the population aspects of development. Population growth takes place within the "family", or the "household", concepts which have fuzzy contours in economics, especially to the extent that they operate mainly outside the market system /Ohlin 1976 p. 147/. To make things worse, the study of the interactions between demography and economics involves two distinct aspects of the household. Children appear on the consumption side of the analysis of the household. They provide utility, they necessitate a readjustment of the basket of goods which a household consumes (including, e.g., consumption goods, investment goods, durable goods, and children), and they may change the time horizon within which a household maximizes. The determinants, then, of population growth, whether they are economic, social or cultural, should be analysed by studying the consumption behaviour of the household.

The change in the consumption side introduced with population growth has an impact on the production behaviour of the household. It changes the relationship between labour and capital endowments, the relationship between leisure and labour, and, through these, it changes the budget constraint of the household. The consequences, then, of population growth should be analysed by studying the production side of the household. Finally, the interrelationships between economic and demographic variables, i.e., the interaction between determinants and consequences of population growth should be studied by combining the consumption and production side of the household within, say, a utility maximization model. The problem is that such an integrated framework of decision-making has not been available in economics.

Another analytical deficiency which has hampered the study of economic-demographic interrelations is that general equilibrium analysis, as opposed to partial equilibrium analysis and comparative statics, is not fully developed in economics. This becomes an even more serious handicap when the general analysis must also include variables which are not strictly economic. General equilibrium analysis can lead to empirical results which are not consistent with the findings of partial analysis. Consider, as an example, the findings of partial regression analysis in which both income and education are negatively related to fertility rates (although the former weakly and rather inconclusively, while the latter may have a U-shape). Yet, on the basis of Hicksian micro-analysis of consumer behaviour, one would have expected that higher incomes by easing the budget constraint, would lead to larger families. The benefit-cost-of-children approach has made lame attempts to solve this conundrum. Within a general equilibrium framework, this oddity can well disappear. Both income and education become endogenous variables which are interrelated and determined though still another set of exogenous variables. In this context, it is possible that the effect of income on both fertility and education is positive, but the latter variable affects fertility negatively, and this explains the inconclusive results obtained through partial analysis. The same problem arises in connection with savings and fertility rates which also yield inconclusive results. Could one assume that family size is the exogenous variable which influences savings rates, or might not both variables be endogenous, and, along with income, be determined by yet another set of variables, among which there are also social and cultural variables? The proper approach would call for estimating the reduced form of the economic-demographic model, in which each endogenous variable is expressed as a function of every exogenous variable.

The handicap of using partial analysis in the place of general analysis is compounded by the fact that disequilibrium analysis, which would have been more appropriate for treating economic-demographic problems, is totally non-existent in economics. The population problem appears in the form of a disequilibrium between birth rates and death rates. This disequilibrium is largely associated with exogenous changes in technology which have not had the chance to work themselves out in a new equilibrium position. In the twentieth century, there has been a dramatic change in the technology of death control. Such technology, being cheap and in harmony with the values and institutions prevalent in most countries, has spread rapidly over DCs and LDCs alike. More recently, there has also been a radical change in the technology of birth control. This, however, has not been in a position to offset the impact of the technlogy of death control for three reasons. First, it followed the advances of medical science by a few decades - which was enough to create a serious backlog problem of population. Second, unlike the technology in death control which can be effectively disseminated and applied by the State, the technology in birth control must be applied at the individual level. This makes it more expensive and more likely to conflict with established value systems which favour high fertility as a means of biological survival when survival probabilities were lower in the past. Third, and quite independently of the value system, the economic system may make high fertility a viable proposition at the family level. This is especially the case in agrarian and traditional societies, and appears in the form of growing (both absolutely and relatively) agricultural populations.

The Focus and Structure of this Report

The 1974 World Population Conference at Bucharest and the 1975 World Food Conference at Rome gave a new impetus to the analysis of demographic problems within a general system of socio-economic transformation. One way of making this concern operational is through studying the interrelationships between demography and economics in the process of development. Global models, in which these interrelationships appear explicitly, will be represented in this report, as well as partial analytical approaches, such as the one treating the effects of nutrition on fertility. The drawback of the existing global models and of the partial approaches is that they rarely include the full chain of causation (e.g. nutrition-fertility - lagged effects on labour force - agricultural production-nutrition-fertility). As mentioned earlier, these spillover effects can be captured only if a general equilibrium system is constructed for the analysis of demography and economics. The construction of such a system is beyond the scope of this Report.

The specific focus of this report is on agriculture. The reasons for this sectoral bias are manifold. Because of its size alone, agriculture is the most important sector in many countries, and in the typical LDC most population growth takes place in the agricultural sector. Demographic variables, as a result, influence the growth and structure of the agricultural sector, including employment, output and productivity. In this perspective, demography is an exogenous variable which interacts with agriculture, and the analysis becomes a special case of the more general theme of the interactions between demography and economics in the process of development.

Agriculture deserves special emphasis in the study of economic-demographic interactions for an additional reason. The literature has consistently singled out the sector as exhibiting a special pattern of demographic behaviour. The relatively high fertility rates of agricultural households can be explained if certain intervening variables which determine demographic behaviour, such as traditionalism, education, etc., are agricultural correlates. If this were the case, the study of agriculture would have already been covered as a special case of the study of the economic-demographic interactions. However, it will be suggested in this report that the causal ordering going from agriculture to demography extends beyond the existence of agriculture-specific values of intervening variables. Agricultural production is organized around a corporate, family-based way of life in which the agricultural households constitute farm-firm complexes combining both production and consumption decisions. Within this institutional framework, there is a definite intergenerational wealth flow which is more pronounced than the similar wealth flow in households which do not operate family farms. It is this characteristic of the sector which is probably at the basis of the distinct fertility behaviour observed in the case of agricultural households.

This special feature of the agricultural sector assumes unique operational significance for the study of economic-demographic interactions. We have already emphasized that the conventional treatment of the topic has suffered from the use of partial approaches which have considered as exogenous the one set of variables be they demographic or economic - while analysing their impact on the other set. The proper approach, however, would be to consider both sets of variables as interdependent and determined within a general framework. This can be best done by studying these interrelations within the micro-economics of the agricultural household which combines both production and consumption decisions. Unhappily, such an integration of the two sides of the agricultural household for the study of economic-demographic interactions has not been attempted in the literature.

Finally, the whole discussion will be referenced to the processes of planning for development in general and for agricultural development in specific. Throughout the Report, and more specifically in the final chapter, the discussion will be referenced to the possible utilization of the resultant insights in order to improve agricultural planning and policy-making. The latter concern can be thought of as having two dimensions. First, there is the extent to which routine agricultural planning and policy-making can be improved by having access to disaggregated demographic information and by utilizing it as suggested by the discussion in this report. Second, there is the extent to which planned agricultural change can be made to contribute to the achievement of objectives in the demographic sector pursued in an economy-wide context. The possible usefulness of global analytical frameworks explicitly depicting demographic-economic interaction will be investigated, though the problem of making agricultural planning demography-responsive encompasses the entire range of global and partial approaches to the area of concern (e.g. the effects of using disaggregated demographic information to demand analysis and projections).

The discussion of these themes although drawing liberally on the existing literature in the field, which it reviews, is basically structured around a number of contributions which, in their totality, compose a major part of the FAO activities financed by UNFPA through the PO2 Project. The authors of these individual sponsored studies contributed the corner-stones and the bricks for this Final Report. The mortar and the design was contributed by the editor, Professor Pan A. Yotopoulos of Stanford University - who in the process may also have taken liberties with the authors' views and therefore wishes to absolve them totally from any responsibility for errors or omissions. In other words, this Final Report can be considered as, at best, a summary of the individual contributions and should not be used as a substitute for the individual papers. These are as follows, and can be obtained on request from FAO.

1. A monograph by Pan A. Yotopoulos, Professor of Economics, Food Research Institute, Stanford University, entitled, "The Population Problem and the Development Solution: Interactions Especially in Agriculture". The purpose of this work was to survey the literature on economic-demographic interactions and to formulate testable hypotheses on demographic and economic development as they refer especially to the agricultural sector. All chapters of this Report, with the possible exception of Chapter V, draw on this contribution.

2. A monograph by Drs. P.G.K. Panikar, T.N. Krishnan and N. Krishnaji, of the Centre for Development Studies, Trivandrum, Kerala, on "Population Growth and Agricultural Development: A Case Study of Kerala". This work is a follow-up of the study by some of the same authors and other members of the Centre for Development Studies on Poverty, Unemployment and Development Policy: A Case Study of Selected Issues with Reference to Kerala, which appeared under the auspices of the United Nations /1975/. The present study delves deeper into the agricultural aspects of the demographic developments in Kerala, and constitutes the basis for Chapter IV of this Report.

3. Both the demographic and the agricultural history of Hungary present special interest for contemporary LDCs. Dr. Rudolph Andorka of the Central Statistical Office of Hungary has contributed a monograph under the title "Long-term Demographic Development in Hungary in a Historical Perspective". It is used for the formulation of some agriculture-specific hypotheses of fertility declines in Chapter IV of this Report.

4. Dr. Naiken, Statistician, Statistics Division, FAO, has contributed a paper entitled, "Demographic Variables in Relation to Planning for Agricultural Development". This paper, along with the paper by Yotopoulos, constituted the background for the proper identification of the variables which enter the measurement of economic-demographic interactions. This is the topic of Chapter II of this Report.

5. Dr. Constantino Lluch, previously of FAO and currently with the Development Research Center of the World Bank, and Mr. Jelle Bruinsma of FAO have contributed a number of papers summarized in the contribution entitled "Development in Dual Economies". This contribution is referred to in Chapter II in connection with the interaction between the agricultural and non-agricultural sector and with migration. A survey paper on the theory of dualistic development, a theoretical paper on development in a segmented economy and the application of the segmented economy model to Pakistan are all summarized in the Lluch-Bruinsma contribution.

6. Professor Oded Stark of Bar-Ilan University, Israel, contributed a paper entitled, "Economic-Demographic Interactions in the Process of Agricultural Development: The Case of Rural-to-Urban Migration, Selected Issues and Some Evidence". This contribution is referred to in Chapters II and IV of this Report, and it provides the basis for looking at migration as a new formulation of the agricultural intensification hypothesis.

7. Professors Christopher Bliss and Nicholas Stern, of the University of Oxford and the University of Warwick respectively, contributed a paper entitled, "Productivity, Wages and Nutrition in the Context of Less Developed Countries". This paper is referred to in Chapter IV, where nutrition is examined as a factor contributing to agricultural development.

8. Dr. Béla Martos of the Institute of Economics, Hungary, with the assistance of Dr. Wuu-Long Lin, Econometrician, FAO, contributed a paper entitled, "Systems Simulation Studies for Long-term Population and Economic Planning". This paper reports on the FAO

Economic-Demographic Planning Model, and is complemented by several other papers on the formulation of this model, and on the testing of the model for Egypt and its application in Pakistan.   Chapter V of this Report presents a summary and a critical evaluation of this model.

9.   Professor Warren Sanderson of Stanford University contributed a paper entitled, "Economic-Demographic Simulation Models: A Review of their Usefulness for Policy Analysis". This contribution has served for the critical evaluation of the Martos-Lin Economic-Demographic Model in Chapter V, as well as for the summary discussion of the Bachue-2 Model, the Simon Model, the Tempo II Model and the Kelley, Williamson and Cheetham Model, also in Chapter V.

10. Dr. Nicholas Alexandratos of FAO contributed part of Chapter V and Chapter VI of this Report which draws together the insights provided by the discussion on the process of agricultural planning and policy-making.   Dr. Alexandratos also served as co-editor of this Final Report, as a coordinator of the various projects under PO2, and as an untiring guide and mediator who assured the proper orientation and the eventual convergence of the contributions reported here.

CHAPTER II

THE DIMENSIONS OF DEMOGRAPHIC ANALYSIS

Both for conceptual discussion and for empirical analysis, it is important to define precisely the variables which will be studied. In the past, the study of demographic factors in relation to economic and social variables has often suffered from incomplete and occasionally incorrect specification of the variables involved. The most conspicuous cases refer to the use of birth rates instead of fertility rates to specify the demographic variable in the analysis, the measurement of employment under assumptions which hold certain demographic conditional variables constant and the treatment of migration which refers both to the demographic and the economic side.

Birth Rates and Fertility Rates

The variable of paramount importance in the specification of the demographic side of the relationship is the population size, and whether this is stationary, increasing or decreasing. A stationary population may be the result either of high birth and high death rates or of low birth and death rates.

The size of population is determined by births, deaths and net migration, and the rate of change in population is determined by the respective time derivatives of these variables. By disregarding migration for the moment, we can define the rate of natural increase in population as equal to the crude birth rate minus the crude death rate. The crude birth rate is defined as the number of births in a year per 1 000 population at mid-year, and similarly the crude death rate is defined as the number of deaths in a year per 1 000 population at mid-year. These rates are useful as indicators of the general level of mortality and fertility. They also indicate the contribution of mortality and fertility to the overall population growth rate.

The contribution in this Report of YOTOPOULOS /1977/ closely examines the basic variables in demographic analysis. For some purposes, viz., the study of the impact of demographic factors on developmental variables, the rate of increase in population and the corresponding crude birth and death rates are the appropriate variables. Population pressure, for example, determines man/land ratios, and, through these (at least partly) the technology which affects development. However, when causality goes the other way, one wishes to examine the family decision-making framework which leads to lower levels of population increase. The specification of the appropriate variables in this case may well need to be different.

Consider first the case of death rates on the assumption that they are independent of birth rates. In recent history, the crude death rates have been decreasing monotonically with time. These declines have been attributed to several factors - improved nutrition; improved communications and transportation facilities which made it easier to combat the spectre of recurring famines; and last, but not least, the development, importation and rapid implementation of modern and relatively inexpensive public health measures and medical technologies. In this sense, declines in crude death rates are at least indirect functions of economic and social development. Still, when one searches for control variables which would decrease the rate of population increase, the manipulation of death rates becomes devoid of real interest. The reason is that, since most people desire long and healthy lives, conscious manipualtion of death rates can lead only to population increases, and not to decreases.

However, the assumption that death rates are independent of birth rates is an over-simplification. The former certainly also reflect the historical record of the birth rates. A history of high birth rates tends to produce a low death rate through its effect on the age structure of the population. For example, Czechoslovakia had a crude death rate of 11 in the fifties. Yet the expectation of life at birth was 62. The number of deaths per 1 000 population was large in Czechoslovakia because, with its history of low birth rates, the country had a high proportion of old people.

A similar problem arises with respect to the birth rate. The birth rate is the result of a combination of several factors: the proportion of women of child-bearing age in total population; the age structure of the women of child-bearing age; the age-pattern of nuptiality; and the age-specific marital (and extramarital) fertility rates. A change in the crude birth rate can be the consequence of a change in one or more of these variables.

However, when decision-making with respect to population is analysed, i.e., when socio-economic influences are studied, the first two of the above variables (the proportion of women of child-bearing age and their age structure) are parameters fixed by historical experience rather than variables subject to behavioural determination. As a result, they should not enter the causal ordering which goes from economic to demographic variables.

Consider the time-profile of a rapidly growing (high fertility, low mortality) population. By definition, it will be a "young population", with, say, 50 percent of the population under twenty which is typical of a large number of LDCs. The number of women entering child-bearing age at any point in time constantly increases, and it is greater than the number of women who leave the child-bearing cohorts. In these circumstances, if the birth rate happens to remain constant, that must imply that there is a smaller number of births per woman of child-bearing age, i.e., that fertility rates have decreased. Even if the birth rate is found to increase, the fertility could still have decreased, depending on the age structure of the population.

Finally, it is not only crude death rates which reflect the experience with crude birth rates, but crude birth rates themselves to a certain extent incorporate the arithmetic of crude death rates. If mortality rates are lowered and hence more infants survive and other people tend to live longer, the effect is to increase the number of persons outside child-bearing age. Unless there are offsetting changes in fertility rates, this effect will appear as an increase in total population, and therefore as a decrease in the crude birth rate. By analogy, one can also describe the situation as regards migration. Emigration, e.g., usually involves people of working, and most probably of child-bearing age, and so tends to reduce the number of births. The converse is the case with immigration.

The point to be emphasized is that both birth and death rates have two components. One reflects exclusively the momentum of the arithmetic of vegetative population growth, and as such refers to the mechanics of constructing model stable populations. No systematic behavioural relationship can be specified to explain this component of crude birth rates. The other component is related, directly or indirectly, to socio-economic variables. The problem is then to redefine a demographic variable which excludes the former part of arithmetic inevitability entering into the definition of crude birth and death rates. This variable should be able to capture directly the impact of socio-economic variables on demographic factors. Should we for this purpose use crude birth and death rates, we are likely to mask the effects of socio-economic variables on demographic factors.

The appropriate variable offering a better measure of the impact of socio-economic factors is a measure of fertility and mortality which controls for the effect of the age composition of the population.[1] An indicator of fertility which also considers the age structure is the general fertility rate (GFR), defined as the number of births per 1 000 women of child-bearing age (generally taken as between 15 to 49).[2] Another more refined fertility measure is the total fertility rate (TFR), which takes into account the age detail of women of child-bearing age. It represents the sum of the age-specific maternal birth rates (number of births per thousand women in specified age groups) over all the child-bearing period. In other words, a total fertility rate of 4.5 per woman means that a hypothetical woman conforming to the age-specific fertility pattern in effect for a current year would have 4.5 children on the average by the time she attained her menopause. In this calculation, the age-specific birth rates for each year receive equal weights.

The corresponding correction of the mortality trends for the age distribution is given by the expectation of life at birth (years), derived from a statistical model known as a life table. The expectation of life at birth is the average number of years which a group of babies could be expected to live if subjected throughout their lives to current mortality risks at each age.

1/ It has, of course, been stressed in the literature that the age composition of the population which enters the birth rate makes that variable less suitable for analysis as compared to the fertility rate: "Like the life expectancy at birth, in the case of mortality it (gross reproduction rate) is the composite expression, in a single measure, of the combined effect of fertility rates prevailing at each age, in complete independence of the composition of the population in regard to sex and age." /Population Reference Bureau 1975, p. 11/. This difference, of course, disappears in the case of stable populations. The problem, however, is precisely that the demographic data with which researchers have been working, specifically those of LDCs, do not come from stable populations. The analyses, therefore, of developmental and demographic interactions which utilize birth rates rather than fertility rates are biased. See, for example, Kirk and Srikanta /1969/, and Anker /1974/.

2/ For more detailed definitions and a fuller discussion of these variants of fertility rates, see Baldwin /1975, p. 36/.

The conclusion of the above discussion is compelling. When one probes for causality going from socio-economic factors to demographic variables, the behavioural equation must be specified in terms of total fertility rates. On the other hand, the level of population is the variable which transmits causality from demographic to economic factors, as, e.g., in studying the population pressure on resources or the employment implications of population growth. The appropriate variable for the analysis in that case is the birth rates.

While birth rates have been commonly used in analyses which treat demographic variables as exogenous and study their economic implications, only rarely have fertility rates been used as the endogenous variable which reflects the impact of social and economic change. A good example of this proposition is the literature on the demographic transition and on fertility differences. The specification of the demographic variable in twelve studies reviewed by the United Nations /1977/ is as follows. The crude birth rate was used in six studies /Boyer and Richard 1975/, /Drakatos 1969/, /Ekanem 1972/, /Farooq and Tuncer 1974/, /Oechsli and Kirk 1975/; children ever born were used in four studies /Cain and Weininger 1973/, /Freedman 1963/, /Snyder 1974/, /Hicks 1974/ the child-woman ratio was used in one study /Kleinman 1973/; a male general fertility rate was used in one study /Heer 1966/; the general fertility rate was used in two studies /Boyer and Richard 1975/, /Guest 1973/, and the total fertility rate in one study /Boyer and Richard 1975/. This misspecification of the demographic variable has biased the results of the studies of causal relationships between the economic and the demographic side. While, for example, the standard conclusion of the literature on the demographic transition is that strictly economic factors do not seem to matter, YOTOPOULOS /1977/, who tested the hypothesis as part of this project (see annex) by using a more appropriate specification of the variables, was able to obtain significant results with the expected coefficient signs by regressing the fertility variable on per capita income and on income distribution in an international sample of 64 countries.

Unemployment as Determined by the Interaction of Economic and Demographic Factors

Demographic Projections as Exogenous Variables in the Study of Development

Basic demographic variables enter directly into the process of planning for economic development. In connection with agricultural sector planning or with perspective studies, for example, the size, structure, and urban-rural distribution of the population play a major role in the determination of the demand for food and agricultural products, and in this way affect the agricultural production targets. Similarly, the agricultural and non-agricultural distribution of the population and labour force determine, to a certain extent, sectoral employment goals or objectives as well as sectoral average incomes. For this purpose, we need only baseline estimates, but also projections of the relevant demographic variables corresponding to the time horizon of the study.

The methodology of demographic projections for development planning received special emphasis in this Project, and its deficiencies in the context of economic-demographic interactions were highlighted /NAIKEN 1977/. Two methods are traditionally used by demographers for these projections. The component method, whereby separate assumptions are made regarding the components of population growth – fertility, mortality and migration – is the commonly used procedure for preparing the total population projections by sex and age. As regards the projections of the other sectoral or subnational population segments, the ratio method is the procedure often used. According to this method, the size of the population in question is obtained by applying suitable ratios to the total or parent population projections. Thus, the total labour force is derived by applying labour force participation rates by sex and age to the corresponding population projections; the urban/rural and agricultural/non-agricultural population dichotomies are derived by applying the ratio of either the urban or the rural population in the total population and the ratio of either the non-agricultural or agricultural population in the total population, respectively, to the total population projections; and the agricultural and non-agricultural labour force segments are obtained by applying the ratio of either the non-agricultural or agricultural labour force in the total labour force to the total labour force projections. Given this methodological framework, the growth of various sectoral or subnational population segments will depend partly on the projected total population growth and partly on the assumed changes in the relevant ratios. The changes in the ratios used for the projections of the urban/rural population and the agricultural/non-agricultural population and labour force mainly reflect the rates of net migration between the relevant segments.

The projections thus derived are used directly in the planning model (whether formal or informal) for considering their implications on demand, employment etc. In other words, the demographic changes are treated as exogenous variables in the planning mechanism.

However, the above approach regarding the incorporation of demographic variables cannot objectively take into account the effects of the economic and social transformation, implied by the planning process, on the relevant demographic factors. Virtually all the factors or ratios on which assumptions are made for projecting the various demographic variables may be either directly or indirectly affected by the economic and social changes resulting from the planning. This points to the need to consider the nature of demographic variables in planning as both determinants and consequences of development. Hence, it is not sufficient to establish assumptions for projections of the demographic variable with regard to one factor at a time or to work with independent assumptions. Rather, we need to consider as endogenous variables in the planning exercise together with other relevant socio-economic variables the various parameters which determine the growth of the relevant demographic variables, namely fertility, mortality, international migration, rural-urban migration, labour force participation rates, and inter-sectoral shifts of population and labour. In other words, there should be a coordinated handling of all important factors simultaneously through a form of system analysis. Such socio-economic-demographic planning models should be capable of illustrating the feedback effects of development plans on the parameters of demographic growth, and hence on the demographic variables themselves.

The Demographic Components of Employment

The measurement of employment and unemployment, especially in the agricultural sector, was examined in detail in this Project /YOTOPOULOS 1977, Chapter VII/ as an example of the interaction between economic and demographic factors. These interactions are usually overlooked, and the result is that errors and ambiguities are introduced in the planning procedures. The problem can be discussed with reference to Figure 1.

It is convenient and customary to distinguish the set of dependents in a population and to define the dependency ratio as the ratio of population under 15 and over 65 to the population in the working age brackets - 15 to 65. This is a purely demographic statistic. Since it is the birth rate which largely determines the structure of the population tree, the relationship between birth rates and dependency ratios is direct. Some typical values of this relationship are /Alexandratos 1975/:

	DCs	LDCs
Population growth rate (percent)	1.0	2.3
Dependency ratio (per 100)	57	80

Both high and low birth rates are associated with high dependency ratios — the former because the population is too young (too many people below 15), and the latter because it is too old (many people over 65).

The population of working age is the starting-point for determining the labour force. It is combined with the objective circumstance of whether one is holding a job or is seeking work, and, expressed as a ratio of a given population group, it defines the participation rate. Given the size and the age structure of the population, the participation rate determines the labour force.

Participation rates vary according to levels of economic development, the type of economic activity, the age-sex composition of the population and other such characteristics. On the average, they range between 0.25 and 0.50 and there exist significant discrepancies as between participation rates for DCs and LDCs between males and females. This deserves further comment in order to demonstrate the ambiguity of labour force statistics /Yotopoulos and Nugent 1976, p. 200/.

A variety of factors, both economic and non-economic, objective and subjective, combine to explain the variation in labour force participation rates. The younger the population (i.e. the higher the proportion of dependents below 15 to total population), the lower the average labour force participation rate. The age composition of the population is then a systematic factor which determines the participation rate. The sex composition introduces another systematic factor. Child-bearing confines women at home for long periods of time. Hence the relationship between female labour force participation and fertility rates is inverse. Non-economic factors, such as social customs and conventions, also tend to reduce the labour force participation of females, especially in LDCs. As incomes rise, more opportunities for female employment will be created outside the household and within the structured labour markets, and this will be recorded as an increase in participation rates. Participation rates, therefore, are among the demographic variables which cannot be projected

Figure 1

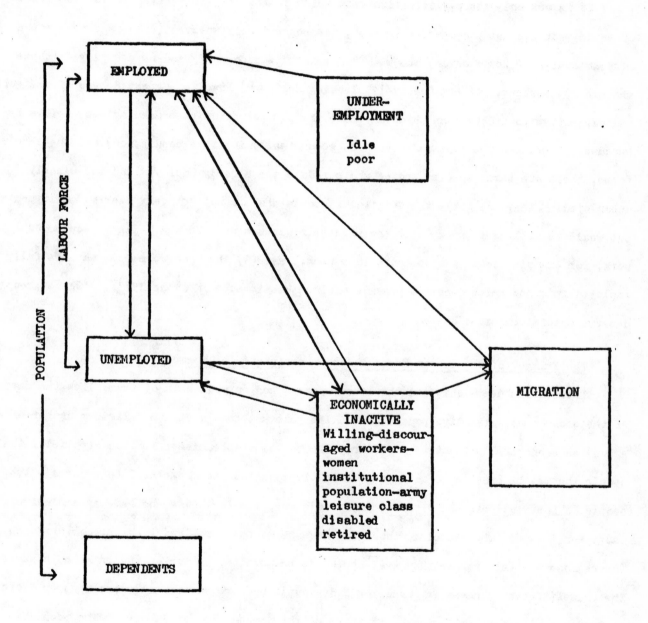

into the future on the assumption that they are exogenous to the level of development. On the contrary, they are determined in the process of interaction between economic and population factors.

It is not only the participation rate which introduces ambiguities in the measurement of employment and unemployment. In fact, the concepts of employed (those who work for a minimum number of hours during the week "in gainful employment") and of unemployed (those who are not working, but are "actively" looking for work) involve a great degree of ambiguity and subjective considerations which may make the participation rate meaningless. This is because, between the dependents (or the economically inactive population) and the labour force, there are three special groups who straddle the already employed and the clearly unemployed. They are: (1) the "willing", people who are not actively seeking employment but would be willing to work under the right circumstances; (2) the "idle", people who work, for example, less than 36 hours in a week; and (3) the "poor", people who are fully employed in a job which does not provide minimum subsistence /Krishna 1973/. These groups deserve special examination.

The Fringes of the Labour Force and the Persistence of Unemployment

Between the dependents and the labour force, and outside both of them, lies the category of the economically inactive population. The relevant box in Figure 1 lists a number of groups as economically inactive. Towards the bottom of the classification are listed the people who may be considered as having definitively withdrawn from the labour force - the people in institutions, the rich who enjoy idleness, the lazybones who have an exclusive taste for leisure, the disabled, those who have permanently retired from the labour force for reasons of taste rather than age, etc. As we move to the top of the ranking, however, the classification changes in favour of individuals who are economically inactive by "forced choice" - a situation which is an attribute of the demand side of labour. The people in "hidden unemployment", for example, or the "discouraged workers", are persons who are outside the labour force, as commonly measured, but who would be willing to enter it if they believed market opportunities were favourable.

The basic reason why discouraged workers are not employed, and are not looking for work is a gap between the wage rate expected from work and the one prevailing in the labour market.

It may well be that the labour demand side is more responsible for that gap. This is the case of groups who face additional barriers to employment. Mothers with young children to care for would have accepted a suitable part-time job if it were available. It is also possible that the supply of labour side is more influential in determining the set of discouraged workers. The mother with young children attaches a high reservation price to her services, and expects to cover at least the cost of the housekeeper or of the nursery needed for her children if she works. Most commonly, it is the combination of demand and supply elements which operates in the case of discouraged workers.

An important group among the discouraged workers are those who can afford unemployment and also have a good reason for entertaining higher expectations from the labour market. They are the young who can still find support within the family, and especially those who are overeducated for the jobs available to them. In a situation of excess supply of university graduates - which is a not uncommon phenomenon today - the student will at first linger on the fringes of the labour force by prolonging his education. Eventually, he will be entering the labour force, and will then be counted as employed (when he will displace marginal workers, if necessary) or as unemployed. In the latter case, measured unemployment will increase. Alternatively, if the discouraged workers enter the labour market and find employment, it is probable that this will not be immediately reflected in a corresponding decrease in the unemployment rate. This is shown in Figure 1 by the arrows going directly to the employment and unemployment sets from the box of the economically inactive. The time taken for the discouraged workers to enter the labour force will depend on the speed of adjustment of their expectations and on the objective improvement of employment opportunities. One way for people in hidden unemployment to seek to improve their opportunities to obtain a job is by migrating to another labour market. The implications of this type of migration - migration which involves this fringe category, rather than the involuntary unemployed - could be profound for the agricultural sector, as we will see below.

Three conclusions emerge from this conceptual examination of hidden unemployment /Yotopoulos and Nugent 1976, p. 202/:

> First, to the extent that the available labour force statistics do not include hidden unemployment, the magnitude and importance of the unemployment problem may have been substantially underestimated. Second, an improvement in the objective labour market

conditions will not be reflected in a decrease in unemployment as long as the new jobs go to people who were previously in the hidden unemployment group. Only the size of the labour force will increase. Third, since the hidden unemployed may consist of individuals with superior education and other background characteristics, it seems likely that it may be these discouraged workers and not the openly unemployed who migrate. If so, the role of migration as an equilibrating force that would tend to drain the pool of the unemployed and equalize wage rates may have been greatly exaggerated.

While the inactive workers represent a potential situation of unemployment, the under-employed workers pose an actual problem. This group consists of people who are technically employed, but not fully so, either because of the duration of work, or because of the efficiency of work, or because of income from work. The criterion of the duration of work applies to people who are in "visible underemployment", i.e., they work part-time or for short periods. Examples are the seasonal occupations and the jobs with pronounced peaks and troughs. If workers fail to meet the criterion of efficiency of work, they fall into the category of disguised unemployment. They may be working full-time, but their job does not permit the full use of their highest existing skills and capacity. In an important group among those people, there is a misfit between education and occupation. The element of underutilization arises in these situations because the occupation is incompatible with the education and training of the worker.

These categories of underemployment have been labelled in Figure 1 as the "idle". They are the workers who could produce more in their employment were the duration and/or efficiency situation better. The "poor" in Figure 1 are the people who may be fully employed, but who do not earn a minimum subsistence from the job /Krishna 1973/. It is the income criterion of employment which is not met in situations such as this. An implication of the poverty content of underemployment is the eixstence of the "additional worker" - the indivi-dual who takes up paid work to supplement family income. A largely untested hypothesis suggests that, as job prospects and family incomes improve, the additional worker will with-draw from the labour force and participation rates will decline. This is shown in Figure 1 the arrow which goes from the employed set to the economically inactive category.

The Demographic Components of Employment Specifically in Agriculture

The previous discussion has touched on the problems of measurement of employment and unemployment in general. These problems are compounded when applied to agriculture. As a

result, ambiguities abound in relation to measuring agricultural employment and underemployment. The following specific sources of confusion can be mentioned /Naiken and Schulte 1976;
Schulte, Naiken and Bruni 1972/.

First, macro-data are more easily available for rural than for agricultural populations,
and, as a result, the two concepts are often confused. Rural population is commonly measured
as the residual of total population minus urban population - which is based on the criterion
of residence. Agricultural population, on the other hand, is defined as the sum of the
persons who have been identified as working or seeking work in agriculture (including
forestry and fisheries) and their non-working dependents. The two concepts of rural and
agricultural populations, as a result, overlap with urban and non-agricultural populations
and their pairwise combinations. It is necessary, therefore, to resort to the application
of the concept of employment in order to derive the estimate of the agricultural population.

Second, the concept of employment is itself involved and complex as the general analysis
above has suggested. It becomes even more tenuous when applied to agriculture because of the
usual mode of operation in that sector of household-firm complexes. Employment is defined
in terms of three components: involvement in actual working or looking actively for work;
involvement in "gainful employment for others' account or on one's own account" (which
includes "assisting" in the production of marketable goods and services); and involvement
extending over a minimum number of hours in the week preceding the census. Among other
problems, the usual ones of "production", "consumption" and "social activities" and that of
how to treat "services" arise when the concept of employment is applied to the agricultural
sector /G.T. Jones 1972, Ch. 1/. Additionally, given the seasonal nature of agriculture,
the duration of work for qualifying a worker as employed or being within the labour force
becomes an issue, and the treatment of family members arises as a special problem. On the
latter question, the international convention is to regard family workers as "unpaid family
workers assisting in the operation of business or farm" as belonging to the labour force,
with the proviso that they work at least one third of "normal hours" /ILO 1976/. This
apparently rules out much of handicraft and building activity, which is performed within the
family system, and as a result escapes the market exchange test.

Given the unavailability of data on agricultural population, estimates of the agricultural population can rely only on the sum of employed and unemployed, i.e., on the concept of the labour force, no matter how ambiguous and incomplete that may be. Naiken and Schulte /1976/ have devised such a method. It is based on estimating the behavioural relationship between agricultural labour force and agricultural population, and using that as a proportionality constant. The assumption is made that the overall participation rates in agriculture and non-agricultural activities are equivalent. One may question the validity of such an assumption on the ground that women and children participate in farm work to a greater extent than they do in non-agricultural activities. However, the result of that bias, on estimating the overall participation rates may be offset by the fact that there is a high proportion of children in agriculture because of higher fertility rates. Furthermore, in LDCs with commonly large agricultural sectors, the measured overall participation rates are likely to reflect more closely the agricultural participation rates, because of the high weight carried by the sector. In any event, the relative stability of the relationship has been established empirically /Schulte, Naiken and Bruni 1972/. Having obtained estimates of the economically active (in agriculture and overall), the authors multiply the inverse of the overall participation ratio (economically active $\div$ total population) by the economically active in agriculture to obtain an estimate of the agricultural population.

The method solves the problem of estimating agricultural population at the expense of lumping together agricultural employment and unemployment and by taking the participation rate as a constant deduced largely from overall economic variables. In agriculture, the concept of (open) unemployment becomes tenuous, and its measurement, for groups other than the landless workers, has questionable relevance. The "labour force" approach commonly applied to measure unemployment has only limited usefulness in agriculture which is organized in farm-firm complexes.[1] In situations of self-employment, the nexus between employer and employee, which, when broken, defines unemployment, does not exist. The condition of "looking for work actively" which defines the unemployed is hardly ever met. The length of the work week depends more on the seasonal labour requirements than on some "normal" standards, and full employment is less of a concern within a household than the attempt to

---

[1] For a comprehensive discussion of the deficiencies of the labour force approach to LDCs, see G. Myrdal /1968, Vol. II, pp. 994 ff./.

share work among the able bodied. A rich literature, as a result, has developed around the concept and the measurement of labour underemployment in agriculture.

We will not review this vast literature here.[1] We will only highlight selective aspects of the duration of work, of the efficiency of work and of the income from work which may have more pronounced demographic implications.

The evidence on agricultural underemployment is based either on the labour force approach or on the labour utilization approach, and suggests that "visible underemployment" on a year-round basis — the situation of people working involuntarily part-time or for shorter periods than they would have wished — is not as serious a problem in family-operated agriculture as was once considered.[2] Actual underemployment is the inevitalbe result of the pronounced cyclical pattern of agricultural activities. The pronounced peak labour requirments of the planting or harvesting season can be met in one (or a combination) of three ways. First, there is the technique of keeping part of the labour force in reserve in visible underemployment during the trough seasons of agricultural activities. Second, one can draw on the economically inactive population in order to meet the peak season labour demands. Third, one can mechanize the operations involved in the peak season activities. Should permanent employment opportunities exist in other sectors, the social cost of maintaining underemployed labour in agriculture to handle peak demands is high. But the third possibility is also costly — that of leaving specialized capital idle for the full year in order to handle the peak season work requirements. A fourth course would be to decrease the specialization of the work force so that workers from other occupations can help ease the seasonal shortages of agricultural labour and so meet the peak labour demands in different sectors at minimal social cost. The benefits of labour specialization in production, long taken for granted, may deserve more careful study in LDCs.

The efficiency-of-work criterion of underemployment and the income criterion have recently been receiving more attention than the duration-of-work criterion. The low productivity in agriculture or the misfit of skills may be responsible for workers working

---

1/ For recent reviews of this topic, see Jones /1972/, especially Ch. 2; /Singh 1974, pp. 707-740/; /Turnham 1971/.

2/ For some evidence on this matter, see Turnham /1971, pp. 61 ff./. One of the earliest empirical studies to question the widespread existence of rural underemployment and disguised unemployment is Pepelasis and Yotopoulos /1962/.

full-time without earning a minimum subsistence.   In fact, overemployment – work longer than the "norm" – may be the initial effect of overpopulation and poverty, as people try to assure subsistence or to maintain the conventional standard of living.   Boserup [1965, p. 45] observed: "... when the growth of population in a given area of pre-industrial subsistence farming results in lower average output per man-hour in agriculture, the reaction normally to be expected would be an increase of the average number of hours worked per year so as to offset the decline in returns per man-hour."

The evidence on participation rates confirms that at low income levels one is more likely to observe agricultural overemployment.   The negative relationship between participation rates in agriculture and income levels was first documented by Chayanov [1925], who explained the non-participation of women and children in the more affluent households as something which could be afforded.   The converse is true for non-agriculture, where in general the participation rate of women has been increasing with the secular increase in incomes, especially for DCs [Boserup 1974].

A comparison of female labour force participation ratios in agriculture and non-agriculture at different levels of development is especially instructive.   Durand [1974] has defined five levels of development based on an index which uses energy consumption per capita and percent share of the non-agricultural sector in total employment of the labour force.   Data on female participation ratios for an international cross-section show that female non-agricultural employment is U-shaped as the level of development increases.   Female agricultural participation rates are consistently lower than non-agricultural ones at all levels of development, with the exception of the lowest, where female participation ratios in agriculture are 50 percent higher than in non-agriculture.   This research should be further pursued with more careful measurement of participation ratios and more representative definitions of the level of development.   It could also be complemented by carefully distinguishing the stages of demographic transition.   It would then be possible to test not only for the relationship between levels of income and female labour force participation in agriculture, but also for the multiple relationship between participation rates, income, and fertility rates.   Elise Boulding [1976, p. 54] has advanced an interesting hypothesis which involves the three variables:

Most of the material on family planning ... (has) made assumptions about women as partners in couple relationships, about the presence of families and about male breadwinners, whereas some of our hardest core food and population problems are in areas where women are heads of households. In Africa, up to 70 percent of the farming is done by women. The picture that we have to build up here is of women producers who are not getting the agricultural assistance that male farmers are getting. These are women who, in some areas, have to spend between two and four hours a day simply carrying water; who spend a minimum perhaps of one hour a day carrying wood for fuel. These are women's jobs. During the planting season, women spend 15 hours a day in the fields on top of their other work. There aren't enough hours in the day for the number of things that have to be done. Country by country, there are numbers of farms where women are carrying heavy work loads unaided. They may be widowed; if they have husbands, these men may be working in the cities or in the mines, on plantations, or they may be cash cropping their own farms. But they are not raising the food; the subsistence patch is woman's work. Any way you look at it, this constant hard core of labour to raise food for subsistence is largely being carried out by women unaided......

There are areas in Africa where anywhere from one-quarter to 40 or 50 percent of the farms are run entirely by women ... then you have to look at the need of the women for extra hands to help her. And so this phenomenon of exhausted women breeding malnourished babies should be identified as a systems process that needs help. Women would surely like to bear fewer babies, but they must breed their own helpers. To offer them contraceptives without offering them at the same time help in the shape of seeds, fertilizer, intermediate-technology tools, and advice, doesn't deal with the problem. Women have to get their work done. Therefore the limitation of family size has to be linked to agricultural aid directed at women.

The hypothesis stated goes beyond the relationship between poverty, participation rates and overemployment. It concentrates on female labour force participation rates, and brings in fertility increases as a means of reducing the amount of work falling on the backs of the bone-weary women in poverty-stricken agriculture. We know of no solid evidence for this hypothesis, but it is certainly worth investigating further. If it is confirmed, it may well suggest that the best contraceptive is the wheelbarrow!

The Dynamics of Labour Transfers Out of Agriculture

The economically inactive, and especially the "discouraged workers" and the workers who are in "hidden unemployment" assume special importance in agriculture because of the organization of the sector in household-firm complexes. Yet the groups of the willing and of the discouraged workers have been largely overlooked in the study of agricultural development.

The reason for this neglect lies in the traditional model of migration which is posited to link the agricultural with the non-agricultural sector. More specifically, a number of "dual economy models" build on the initial disequilibrium between agriculture and non-agriculture and describe how equilibrium is being restored, primarily through labour transfers.

Underlying this analysis is a particular view of how the labour market works. It is based on the assumption that it is the marginal workers who are transferred, that is, who migrate.

Agriculture is assumed to employ large numbers of low-wage workers and non-agriculture small numbers of higher-wage workers. The marginal workers transfer out of agriculture, thus increasing wages and per capita incomes in the low-wage sector. At the same time, they increase the supply of labour to the high-wage sector thus reducing wages and per capita incomes there. Through the levelling force of migration, the dualistic features of the economy atrophy and agriculture becomes appended to non-agriculture in terms of rates of growth and development potential. This marks the end of the dual economy.

This description applies to the most common view of dualism, which is essentially an optimistic and unfulfilled theory. The literature on dualism has proliferated since the middle-fifties, and alternative specifications have yielded alternative results which have been summarized and compared in one of the contributions to this project /Lluch 1976/. More specifically, the disequilibrium aspects of trade referring to the open economy were noted in the original contributions of Lewis /1954, 1958/. Foreign trade, according to Lewis, is first and foremost trade in reproducible capital, and it provides the vehicle for expansion of the capitalist sector in the world economy. Through trade, reproducible capital can be put into operation abroad, and a higher surplus obtained than at home, for reasons connected with labour availability at lower wages in LDCs, possible specific natural resource endowments, and above all the existence of institutions favourable to capitalist development.

> The ugly possibility of perennial dualism on a world-wide basis raises its head in Lewis' exposition; capital exports may well be positively associated with the level of capital in the receiving country. If this is so, the wage gap between countries with and without surplus labour would increase. To those who have capital, more capital is given, and the tendency for wages to rise is then stronger /Lluch 1976, pp. 10-11/.

A similar, although stronger argument about the disequilibrating aspects of international trade has been made by Arghiri /1972/.

It is particularly tempting to apply the same analysis to the rural-urban dichotomy in a closed economy and to search for mechanisms which might induce similar disequilibrating features. Two avenues are followed in this direction. First, the notion of the dual econonomy is supplemented by the concept of fragmentation, i.e., sector-specific and non-tradable resource endowments. Second, migration is analysed within an agriculture-specific framework. This becomes necessary because the traditional view of migration in the context of the dualistic development literature as a mechanism which tends to restore equilibrium in the long-run is not congruent with at least three phenomena consistently observed in recent historical experience. First there are generally high rates of migration from the agricultural to the non-agricultural sector. Second, these migration flows persist unabated despite the fact that unemployment in the urban areas tends to increase. Third, despite the high unemployment rates, the wage differentials between agriculture and non-agriculture are maintained, if not increased, and the sectoral dualism becomes accentuated.

Dualism with Market Segmentation

The salient characteristic of LDCs is a low level of income per capita and a large share of agriculture, both in employment and output. A problem, therefore, which assumes centre stage in the study of development refers to the changes in the agricultural sector which are related with growth in per capita incomes. This raises the question of sectoral interdependences and of structural transformation. One specific way - the earliest in post-war development economics - of analysing this problem is through the approach of dualistic economic development.

At the minimum, any economic specification of the concept of dualism involves distingui-shing two sectors along differences in their respective production functions.[1] The sectoral specification, for example, may include a capitalist sector (non-agriculture) which uses reproducible capital and labour and pays the factors on the basis of their respective marginal productivities, while the subsistence sector (agriculture) uses land and labour, and the workers earn subsistence incomes which are considered to be close to the conventional minimum standard. Capital accumulation in the capitalist sector (which is partly financed through the creation of "agricultural surpluses") leads to an increase in the demand for labour, which is drawn out of agriculture. As this process continues, neoclassical economic theory takes over to the point where labour in agriculture is also paid its marginal product, capital eventually flows into agriculture too, and the marginal returns to all factors are equalized in all uses. This is the "break-out" point of economic development. Labour is therefore

---

[1] Non-economic formulations of dualism are often based on other than production-function characteristics. See Yotopoulos and Nugent /1976 p. 253 ff./.

the bridge to economic development, but partly also it is comprised of "surpluses" transferred out of agriculture /Lewis 1954, 1958/; /Jorgenson 1969/,· /Ranis and Fei 1961/.

Several variations on this theme have appeared in the literature, including attempts to cast sectoral dualism in terms of income /Sato and Niho 1971/ instead of output; to introduce agricultural marketable surplus instead of agricultural output /Zarembka 1970/; to introduce differences in sectoral consumption functions in addition to the difference in production functions /Kelley, Williamson and Cheetham 1972/; and to open up the economy by introducing a third export sector /Inada 1971/.

The contribution of this Project to the theory of dualistic development /LLUCH and BRUINSMA 1977/includes the features of dualism in production and consumption patterns which were already incorporated in the literature, plus a notion of segmentation in the factor markets.   More specifically, prices are commonly thought of as performing two functions – an allocation function, related to factor markets, and a distribution function, related to output markets.[1] In the static version of the model, the former function of prices is abrogated.   As a result, labour and capital become sector-specific factors, equilization of factor rewards across sectors is ruled out, and, in the extreme case of segmentation at least and on the assumption that production factors are fully employed, sectoral physical output is exogenously given once the level of technology has been determined.

The distributive function of prices, however, is in operation, and exchange on the output side determines the monetary equilibrium.   Exchange is therefore carried out for consumption and investment purposes, and the equilibrium price and income are such that the output supplies are in fact demanded.   For each sector, there is a consumption function, and consumption demand is estimated within a linear expenditure system, with disposable income as an independent variable.   In such a system, part of the disposable income is spent on given minimum required quantities of each good ("subsistence quantities"), and the remainder of disposable income ("supernumerary income") is allocated over savings and the consumption of each commodity, in shares specific for each income group.   The subsistence commodities are demanded regardless of prices, whereas savings and the balance of consumption are price-sensitive.

---

[1] For a similar disequilibrium approach to agricultural growth see Mundlak /1977/.

This is briefly the static formulation of the model. The segmentation framework is relaxed in the dynamic formulation of the model, which reintroduces to a certain extent the allocative function of prices. More specifically, besides the change in the population of a sector due to the natural population growth, migration can also take place, and, as a result, factors are no longer fully sector-specific. Migration is in fact determined by the disparity between rural and urban incomes, i.e. by wage differentials, differential rates of unemployment and expectations. Similarly, intersectoral movements of capital can also occur in the dynamic model.

If exchange and trade can indeed become a disequilibrating mechanism, one would expect that the application of a segmented economy model would give results which differ from those of a model incorporating the allocative function of prices as well. For illustrative purposes, a numerical analysis for the Pakistani economy was carried out with data for 1967-75, and the model was run at annual intervals over 25 years.

The results of the simulation were compared with the "standard path" of the Pakistani economy as estimated from structural change characteristics /Chenery and Syrquin 1975/ over the income levels modelled for that period. In general, the result of the segmentation is to accentuate the structural change characteristics of the economy. The structural features of the economy can be summarized as follows. An increasing urban population share is accompanied by a persistent high migration (induced by a deteriorating income distribution between the rural and urban sector) and by a high urbanization rate (with a peak increment of 4.74% in the period 1976-80). The income ratio deteriorates because of price and quantity effects, the terms of trade decline, and rural production lags behind urban production. The slower pace at which production in rural areas grows is in turn a consequence of a smaller growth of population (and thus of the labour force), and - in later periods - of the stock of capital goods, combined with differences in productivity (technology). The share of urban output in national income rises steadily. There is a considerable increase in "rural marketable surplus" (rural output not consumed by rural consumers as a percentage of total rural production). (Consumption of rural goods as a share of total private consumption declines sharply - from 61% to 38%.) Finally, GDP per capita, and also per capita expenditure, grow at a rather low rate, and it is the urban income group alone who benefits from this increase, since rural income per capita remains almost constant during the simulation period.

The results of the simulation of the Pakistan economy cannot be considered as very novel and need not be described here in detail. (Indeed sensitivity analysis in most cases confirms the findings of Kelley, Williamson and Cheatham /1972/.) However, some comments are called for on the results on the demographic parameters, i.e., changes in the rural and urban population growth rates and participation rates and variations in the rate of migration. Population growth inevitably leads to an increase in the labour force and to parallel increases in participation rates, and thus affects production. Population growth also increases the number of consumers. Besides this quantity effect on consumption, there is a "price-income" effect which is difficult to predict.

One striking result is the fact that the well-known adverse influence on GDP per capita is attenuated after 1980 in the case of rural population growth. On the other hand, urban population growth has a positive impact on GDP per capita. This is presumably because the economy is particularly sensitive to the urban labour participation rate.

With an increased rural participation rate, the rural-urban income ratio improves, and so curbs migration, and therewith the urbanization process. With an increased rural population growth, in spite of a deteriorating income disparity (and thus an accelerated migration), rural population growth outweighs migration, and the level of urbanization therefore falls. This last proposition can be reversed for urban population growth. In all cases the urban output share falls at an increasing rate. In the case of rural parameter changes, this may be due to quantity effects, since the internal terms of trade turn against the rural sector, but rural physical production is stimulated. As against this, with increased urban population growth, the improvement in the terms of trade enables the rural sector to gain in value terms over the urban sector, although, in terms of physical production, the result is not clear. In all cases, the share of private consumption (and therefore of private savings) in GDP is hardly affected.

The question that arises is why the model has not captured more basic features of the development process. One cannot help thinking that the paucity of data on the Pakistan economy severely restricted the possibilities for calibrating the model. It is necessary

that the structure of the economy be based on better empirical evidence, and probably lags
also should be taken into account.   Also one could think of other refinements and different
sector identification that would improve the results, allowing for example for intersectoral
investment in the dynamic model and allowing for non-tradable production in the agricultural
sector.   Similarly, segmentation of product markets and the absence of price equalization
throughout the economy, may prove to be an important aspect of dualism.   A final conjecture
on the results of the model refers to the way it was estimated.   There are two extremes in
the range of segmentation that one can distinguish.   At one extreme, physical output is
exogenously given and not influenced by prices.   At the other extreme the segmentation model
converges with the neoclassical model if the dynamic adjustments that open up the markets
were introduced often enough.   The conjecture is that by estimating the model in one-year
periods, its dynamic features offset the effects that segmentation introduced in the static
version of the model.

A view of Migration Specific to the Agricultural Sector

We have already mentioned that the conventional treatment of migration fails to explain
a good deal of recent historical experience.   Another failure of the existing migration
framework is that it is general.   It could apply to any individual or to any sector of the
economy.   Yet the strongest migration movement is out of agriculture or from the rural to the
urban areas.   A contribution to this Report /STARK 1977/ proposed to build a framework for
analysing migration as an agriculture-specific phenomenon, and to examine the evidence relating to this new approach.

The specific characteristic of agriculture which has received emphasis in this Report
is the organization around the household-firm complex, within which decisions of consumption
and production take place.   Migration is one of the demographic phenomena which has both
consumption and production overtones, takes place within the household-firm unit, and is,
therefore a family, rather than an individual, decision.   Thus, a starting point, is a
family (rather than individual) utility maximization approach.   Net utility is defined in
the usual terms as the difference between the labour-income utility and the effort-disutility of
work.   The former is assumed to be monotonically increasing with food, and the latter monotonically increasing with labour - their second derivatives being negative.   Given this

specification, the net utility of the household is subject to two "compositional changes" (fertility decisions being exogenous in the model). First, given the family size, the change in the family's age structure results in greater food requirements. This in itself raises the marginal utility from food throughout. Second, family size itself changes over time as additional children are brought into the world. Since the total utility to be derived by a family unit from any given quantity of food cannot be determined independently of the number of its members and since the appropriate assumption is that the relationship between the two is an inverse one, an increase in a family's size thus brings about a downward shift of the utility function. The combined impact of the two compositional changes is thus "a downward projection and twist" - a change in level (intercept) and a change in the rate of change of level (slope). The obvious implication, in a utility-disutility plane, is the achievement of a new "labour equilibrium input" with a lower net utility.

This compositional change in the utility of the household-firm, which occurs because of the "vegetative growth" (age structure) and of the fertility growth in the family, sets in motion the mechanism for the introduction of technological change. Technology and labour are the two arguments in the production function. This view of technological advance is parallel to Boserup's /1965/ view of the intensification of agriculture as a result of population pressure. The only difference is that, in the present context, the dyanmics of the age structure of the household are also considered through the food requirements.

It takes an agricultural surplus to finance technological change. But, if the family is initially endowed with the "cruel parameter" of only a small holding, and average capacity to generate surplus is directly proportional to on-the-farm food production but inversely proportional to the (standardized) number of family consuming members, the prevailing surplus and the expected surplus are likely to be low. Furthermore, in a world of fragmented capital markets,[1] the surplus requirements of the new technology must be met from within the household-firm. This is on the supply side. On the demand side, any surplus which the household can accumulate would be invested in the assets which have the highest rate of return.

---

[1] See McKinnon /1973/ for the analysis and for the evidence Dantwala /1966/, Vasthoff /1968/, Reserve Bank of India /1969, Ch. 18/, Oweis /1972/, Pandey /1972/, Dell'Amore /1973/, Agency for International Development /1973/.

These include physical assets and technological investment on their own farm. Such investments, however, have a certain lumpiness which places a strain on household firms with limited savings, and the fragmented capital markets rule out borrowing. The alternative is investment in financial assets, such as bank deposits, which, however, have low, or even negative government-controlled interest rates. The in-between alternative in which yields are higher than financial assets, but lower than physical capital is investment in human capital, such as education or migration. The scope for migration, therefore, enters the model through the fragmented capital markets - fragmented investment opportunities within which the household firm operates. The purpose of migration is to serve as an intermediate investment, the returns to which are eventually to be reinvested in physical capital in the process of the technological change of agriculture.

Given the migration strategy for the accumulation of surplus for technological change, the selection as to which household member migrates involves three variables: efficiency (productivity) in on-the-farm food production; probability of securing urban employment; and urban wage rate (or urban income in general) once employment has been secured. On the basis of these considerations, the maturing son becomes the prime candidate for migration selectivity.

Compared with his maturing son who either did not participate in agricultural production, or did so but only for a short period, the head of the family is most probably the better farmer. He is more likely to command a good level of husbandry which presumably depends greatly on both tradition and personal past experience ("on the job training"), the first being fully grasped through the latter. His choice of enterprises and practices, timing of operations and general management of farm production can be expected to be nearer to their optimum levels (that is, given the overall set of production constraints).

The reverse seems to hold with regard to production efficiency in the urban sector. Some form of (general) education (e.g. basic skills of communication and computation, sometimes enriched by some vocational training) is a more likely prerequisite for performing a wide range of urban jobs. The maturing son is more likely to possess a given (or often simply any) level of education.

Education is important, both on the supply and on the demand side of the labour market.

On the former, education furnishes the worker with job information which is more (as it is scarce) and better (as it is not of a uniform quality). As a result, more urban labour markets become accessible to him. Education is also a critical determinant of employability on the demand for labour side. Employers are both interested in the substantive content of education to the extent that it enhances the employee's productive potential, and also because they use educational attainment as the best single indicator of the desirable characteristics of potential employees.

The Evidence on the Agriculture-Specific Migration Model

There are three empirical propositions which set this agriculture-specific migration model apart from the main stream of the migration literature. First, and most important, migration is a mechanism associated with technological change in agriculture. Second, technological change is preceded by a constant flow of remittances to the migrant's agricultural household-firm. Third, the migrants come from the well-qualified inframarginal agricultural workers, or else from the "willing workers" of the agricultural sector who were at the fringes of the labour market. This third proposition has an implication with respect to the period of unemployment which the migrant will spend in the urban sector before he obtains a job (short) and with respect to the characteristics of the typical migrant (young, single, and relatively more educated and skilled than the other members of his family and than the typical marginal urban worker).

The study proceeds to review the evidence related to these propositions. Much of this evidence is "softer" than what would have been required to build a solid foundation for the hypothesis. This should not come as a surprise. Four reasons account for the scarcity of evidence, both relating to migration and to technological change at the family farm level. First, the rural-end technological implications of rural-to-urban migration have not been incorporated in most migration models. Consequently, evidence bearing on this issue has not been collected. Secondly, too many migration studies are based on information supplied solely by the migrants. Clearly, the migrant himself, who is located in the urban sector, is not in the best position to inform a researcher whether the ensuing rural-end technological change has been carried out. Thirdly, there is a likely time gap between migration and shift of technology. The interrogation of migrants or even of their rural families too soon after migration will most probably fail to reveal the existence of the postulated sequence. Fourthly, data are too often aggregated at the rural community level rather than given for the individual family farms. The result (since decomposition back to farm level data is out of the question) is that it is not possible to infer that those families within the community who have experienced migration are also the very ones who have undergone the change in production technology. Hundreds of Indian village studies conducted in the early sixties provide striking examples of these shortcomings.[1]

Of special interest is the model's proposition relating to unemployment. The incidence of unemployment among rural-to-urban migrants should be low and the duration of urban unempoyment of rural migrants should be short. Otherwise, the move is likely to deplete the family's small surplus, and thus postpone the technological shift in agriculture. This prediction flies in the face of the conventional interpretation of the evidence summarized in the following statements: "chronic urban unemployment emerged" as a result of a "high rate of rural-urban migration" /ILO 1975, p. 2/; "rural-urban migration is inextricably entwined with the urban employment problems that have accompanied it" /Barnum and Sabot 1976/ "rural-urban migration was proceeding at a rapid rate in most /developing/ countries around the world, only to pile up in the large cities as unemployed or underemployed masses" /Schuh 1976/. The trouble about this view of the link of migration and unemployment are based on the misinterpretation of the evidence.

In order to confirm that it is the migrants who preponderantly form the urban unemployed, one would have to subdivide unemployment data relating to migrants and to non-migrants. The conclusion from studies lending themselves to such a subdivision is that, as a rule, the urban unemployment rate of rural-to-urban migrants is lower than the average unemployment rate. Furthermore, the waiting period of rural migrants seeking urban employment is relatively short. These findings are indirectly supported by studies focusing on the educational profile of the urban unemployed which conclude that a major component of the unemployed is the growth of relatively highly educated persons, only a few of whom are migrants of rural origin.

---

[1] These and other village studies have been collected within the framework of the Village Studies Programme of the Institute of Development Studies, University of Sussex.

In this respect, the unpublished results of the 1973 migration survey in Indonesia deserve some attention /STARK 1977/. They indicate that "over 90 percent of migrants who arrived in Jakarta recently reported themselves to be at least as well off as before migration". The 1972 urban unemployment survey referring to recent migrants (those who came to the city during the preceding year) found that the rate of unemployment for the migrant group - especially for those coming from rural areas - was only slightly higher than that of the natives (13.85 and 10.72 percent respectively) - and this, in spite of the fact that some of the migrants "may have arrived only few weeks/months before the date of the interview". The study also points out that, based on a number of alternative measures, the difference between relevant urban and rural wage rates for migrants is slight. Hence, "the most important factor contributing to migration to urban areas" is the employment differential. Summarizing the evidence, the study asserts that "unemployment in Jakarta cannot be attributed wholly or even mostly to inflow of migrants ... The evidence warrants rejection of the ... hypothesis that migrants come to the city in search of well paid urban industrial jobs and choose to remain voluntarily unemployed for long periods of time".

The empirical evidence presented in relation to this agriculture-specific model of migration leads us to question certain of the common features of parallel work in the literature. If the migrants are not the marginal workers or the unemployed of the agricultural sector, the first impact of migration would be a decrease in the average product of labour in agriculture - rather than an increase, as is usually posited. The migrants do not join the queue of the unemployed in the urban sector, and await their turn to occupy a job in a semi-random process of job allocation /Todaro 1969/. On the contrary, in a systematic process, they are among the first to obtain the new jobs created, or they displace less qualified workers from an existing job. Where this filtering-down of skills takes place, hard-core unemployment in the urban sector increases.

These effects of migration are contrary to the mechanism which equalized wage rates and incomes in the two sectors traditionally associated with the phenomenon. The initial impact of migration is the converse. Migration is therefore a disequilibrium process. In the long-run, however, through the agriculture-specific feature whereby it induces and finances technological progress migration can turn into an equilibrating mechanism.

CHAPTER III

THE INTERACTIONS AND THE ISSUES

A large literature has already accumulated which relates population to development. We will make no attempt to summarize it here; we will merely highlight the basic issues.[1]

Historically, the discussion of the interactions between population and development has followed certain definite cycles. The study of the consequences of population growth attracted interest first, Malthus being among the earliest contributors. He predicted a low level of income equilibrium as the result of population growth. The next step in the historical sequence was the theory of demographic transition. It gave an optimistic outlook to development by shifting the discussion to the determinants of population growth: the increase in European income levels which followed the Industrial Revolution was responsible for dramatic declines in mortality and later for decreases in fertility. The relationship between income and fertility, which Malthus posited as direct, was therefore reinterpreted as inverse.

The discussion of the consequences, as well as of the determinants of population growth, expanded to include other intermediate variables relating to demographic behaviour and economic development. A contribution to this report [YOTOPOULOS 1977] reviews the various relationships identified in this literature and proposes a general framework for analysing the interactions between population and development within a household utility maximization model which incorporates both the production and the consumption decisions of the family. This framework can become readily operational for the study of the agricultural household, since there the farm-firm is the single locus where both the production and the consumption decisions take place.

---

[1] For comprehensive summaries of the contributions to this topic, see, among others, Research Triangle Institute [1971] and McGreevey and Birdsall [1974].

The Consequences of Population Growth

Table 3.1 sketches out, through a set of intermediate variables, two consequences which can lead alternatively to a direct or to an inverse relationship between population growth and incomes. The first views population growth as a stimulant to economic develop-ment, and is identified with the writings, among others, of Hansen /1939/, Hirschman /1958/, Boserup /1965/, and more recently Simon /1976/. Viewed from the perspective of a single equation, partial analysis, the underlying rationale for this sequence is the existence of deficiency of demand. By stimulating demand, population growth provides economies of scale, increases the profitability of investment and the incentive to invest, and gives a further inducement for technological change, an expansion of education, and the qualitative improve-ment in the labour force.

The alternative prospect presented in the lower half of Table 3.1 rests on the implicit hypothesis of shortage of supply. It is associated with the early model-building work of Coale and Hoover /1958/ and the early theoretical work of e.g. Nelson /1956/ and Leibenstein /1954/, among others. A large number of more recent studies converge in viewing population growth, if not as an absolute obstacle, at least as a non-trivial deterrent of economic development for contemporary LDCs. The sequence goes through the availability of decreasing savings although, surprisingly, the compelling evidence on this issue is sparse, with at best only indirect evidence within a one-equation partial equilibrium system, e.g. Leff /1969/, and is reflected in lower investment expenditures and in a decrease in capital/labour ratios. Furthermore, the composition of investment also changes, as a result of population growth, in favour of a higher share of demographic investment and other social overhead capital which makes a lower contribution to direct increases in productivity. The result is an eventual pressure upon the levels of per capita income. Or at least per capita income does not increase as fast as would have been needed in order to reduce poverty substantially. It is now a widely accepted conclusion, King /1974/, that rapid population growth and an ever-expanding labour-force make it almost impossible to relieve unemployment and poverty. They make it difficult to expand education and other social services for the eventual alleviation of poverty. And finally, at the family disaggregation level, since the poorest families have relatively higher fertility rates, rapid population growth makes it difficult to reach effectively the family units which are the prime targets in any attempt to alleviate poverty.

This discussion leads to the second-round effects of the sequence population growth-lower per capita incomes, which are sketched out in the bottom of Table 3.1.[1] Population growth increases future expenditures on education with a very short lag of 5 to 6 years. It also increases expenditures on health more than proportionally to the increase in population, since children and pregnant women are heavier consumers of health services than the typical member of the population. If we control for the state of technology, population growth, by cutting the availability of savings and capital and by increasing the labour force, reduces the ability of the economy to absorb labour and to lower unemployment. This, of course, assumes that population growth did not provide a stimulus for the development of labour-intensive technologies – a proposition which may be feasible in the fifteen or so years which it takes the new increments of population to enter the labour force. Besides making it more difficult to effectively reach the target families with a view to improving income distribution, the relationship between income distribution and population growth is one of the former determining the latter, and it will be examined below. Finally, the relationships between population growth and rural-urban migration, food, resources and environment, and housing, although they should conceptually be uniformly negative, have not been convincingly identified in the literature.

The Determinants of Fertility

While the study of the consequences rightly focuses on population growth, the determinants of demographic change must be studied with reference to fertility rather than to population. The reason for this, as mentioned in Chapter II, lies in the importance assumed by the historical record of population growth (as reflected in the age distribution of population) in determining the population size when the rate of fertility is given.

The empirical research into the determinants of fertility has been carried out at the micro and at the macro-level. Table 3.2 gives the sign for household fertility behaviour with regard to a number of intervening social and economic variables. This table is based on McGreevey and Birdsall /1971/, and the reader is referred to that source for further commentary and for the list of the empirical studies which have been abstracted. A detailed

[1] For a concise discussion from which we borrow see King /1974, pp. 23-24/ and Nancy Birdsall and Rashid Faruqee /1977, p. 22 ff/.

Table 3.1

Alternative Sequences Tracing the Consequences of Population Growth on Economic Development

Independent variable	Nature of relationship with/and		
	Intermediate variable	Dependent variable	Second-round effects
Population growth	+ Stimulus on demand + Incentives to invest + Economies of scale in production + Technological change + Education + Improvement of labour force	+ Per capita income	
Population growth	- Savings - Investment size - Investment composition (i.e. more demographic invest.) - Flexibility in capital/labour and output/input ratios	- Per capita income	- Education - Health-nutrition - Labour force absorption - Income distribution ? Rural-urban migration ? Food ? Resources and environment ? Housing

Note: (+) symbol is used for direct relationship with population growth;
(-) for inverse relationship; (?) for indeterminate relationship;
and (0) for no relationship to fertility.

Table 3.2

Nature of Relationships of Socio-Economic
Determinants of Fertility: Micro Studies

Independent variable	Sign of the relationship	Adequacy of Research
Income	?	Fair
Income distribution	−	Poor
Socio-economic status	−	Poor
Education and literacy		
Female	−	Good
Male	+ or 0	Fair
Employment		
Male	+ or 0	Fair
Female	−	Fair
Rural	+ or 0	Fair
Urban	−	Fair
Children	+	Poor
Age at marriage	−	Poor
Costs of children	−	Fair
Son preference	− or 0	Poor
Infant mortality	+	Good
Urban/rural differentials	0	Fair
Religion	0	Poor

Note: (+) symbol is used for direct relationship with population growth;
(−) for inverse relationship; (?) for indeterminate relationship;
and (0) for no relationship to fertility.

Source: McGreevey, William P. and Nancy Birdsall /1971/. The Policy
Relevance of Recent Research on Fertility. Washington, D.C.:
The Smithsonian Institution, Table 5, p. 65.

discussion of the relationships in the table appears in the contribution to this Report by
YOTOPOULOS [1977]. We can summarize the findings by suggesting that the relationships which
appear the strongest ones in a single-equation-framework analysis are those with female
education (negative), and with infant mortality (positive). The relationship with the size
of income is rather indeterminate, and this is probably due to the fact that, in a single
equation, one cannot separate the pure effect of income on fertility (which must conceptually
be positive) from the price effect (which may be negative) and from the effects of other
correlates of income such as education which are mostly negative. Income distribution may
in time prove a variable which has a definite relationship with fertility, but empirical
research on the topic is at present minimal, and the negative relationship is not well
documented. The relationship between fertility and female employment is also too complicated
to be readily analysed in a single-equation system. When female employment is a correlate
of better education, its impact on fertility is certainly negative. Low-paying female employment or female employment on the farms may on the other hand be positively associated with
fertility, since children yield a direct benefit in that they ease the strain on overworked
mothers by helping with farm work and other activities.

The macro-analysis is based on international cross-sections and/or time series. A
summary of these studies is provided by Birdsall and Faruquee [1977], and is reproduced in
Table 3.3. Most of these studies are based on regression analysis, and at least implicitly
impute causality between certain socio-economic variables and demographic indicators, usually
the birth rate. We have already remarked in the previous chapter that the birth rate is
the wrong variable for describing relationships which go from social and economic variables
to demographic characterestics. If this is correct, the relationships in the table cannot
be interpreted as describing demographic determinants. In a departure from the regression
analysis technique, Oeschli and Kirk [1975] have attempted, with data from Latin America and
the Caribbean, to construct a number of indicators describing the typical profile of a country
at certain stages of the demographic transition. They conclude that the experience of
marked fertility declines is associated, among other things, with literacy rates of 78 percent;
an expectation of life at birth of 60; a primary school enrolment ratio of 65 percent; a
labour force in non-agriculture of 52 percent; an urbanization rate of 40 percent; and a

secondary school enrolment ratio of 22 percent.

The one conclusion to be drawn from this brief review of the literature on the consequences and determinants of population growth is that the analysis must take place at a more disaggregated level and that the issue must be studied within a general framework, as opposed to the partial analysis approach. The following chapter refers to a sectoral disaggregation of economic demographic relationships by dealing specifically with agriculture.

Table 3.3

Nature of the Relationships between Socio-Economic
Indicators and Demographic Transition
(declines in birth rates or fertility rates)

Studies	Data	Variables and sign of correlation coefficient 1/	
Heer /1966/	41 nations, fifties	Per capita income	−
		Newspapers per thousand (education)	−
		Infant mortality	+
		Population density	−
		Increase in energy consumption 1937-53	+
Weintraub /1962/	30 nations, fifties	Per capita income	+
		Proportion population on farms	+
		Infant mortality rate	+
Adelman /1963/	37 nations, 1950	Per capita income	+
		Literacy/newspapers per thousand (education)	−
		Labour force outside agriculture	−
		Population density	−
Kasarda /1971/	50 nations, 1930-1969	Female employment:	
		Unpaid family workers	?
		self-employed	?
		employed for wages or salaries	−
		Urbanization	−
		Industrialization	−
		Education	−
Ekanem /1972/	24 nations (all developing), fifties, sixties	Per capita income	−
		Percent illiterate	+
		Labour force in agriculture	+
		Percent urban	−
		Infant mortality rate	+

Table 3.3 continued

Studies	Data	Variables and sign of correlation coefficient 1/	
Janowitz [1973] 2/	17 nations	Illiteracy	+
		Per capita income	+
		Mortality	?
Bell [1976]	146 nations	Life expectation at birth	+
		GNP per capita 3/	−
Cain and Weininger [1973]	Regions within US	Income of males	+
		Market wage available to women	−
		Education of females	−
		Percent males in high status occupations	−
		Percent Catholic	?
		Wages of domestic help	−
Adelman and Morris [1966]	55 developing nations, 1957-62	Factor I: transformation of social values	*
		Factor II: political values	
		Factor III: nature of leadership	
		Factor IV: social and political stability	
King [1974]	64 nations	Per capita income	−
		Life expectancy	−
		Newspapers per thousand	−
		Distribution of income	−
YOTOPOULOS [1977]	64 countries	Per capita income	−
		Income distribution	−

Note: * Many variables for each factor; see article.

1/ Not all variables were statistically significant at 5 percent level in all studies. See studies for more exact results.

2/ Results varied by different country groups.

3/ Above a threshold level, correlation is negative.

Source: Nancy Birdsall and Rashid Faruqee [1977], Population-Development Relationships: Approaches to Analysis, The World Bank, Population and Human Resources Division (mimeo).

CHAPTER IV

AGRICULTURE-SPECIFIC ASPECTS OF ECONOMIC-DEMOGRAPHIC INTERACTION

The basic target of the research reported here is the economic-demographic interactions in the agricultural sector. The size and importance of the agricultural sector in most LDCs is an obvious reason for this bias. There are other characteristics of agriculture which can justify this sectoral orientation.

The demographic patterns observed in agriculture are indeed different from the other sectors of the economy. It is conceivable that the higher fertility rates of agricultural households are the result of intervening variables which are agricultural correlates – levels of income, educational levels, female labour force participation, the production contribution of children, life expectancy and death rates, etc. The study of these intervening variables, in that case, would have sufficed to capture the demographic behaviour of the agricultural sector. There is, however, more characterizing the agricultural household than could possibly be described by these intervening variables. The operation of the household as a farm-firm combining production and consumption decisions is a characteristic which becomes crucial for the analysis of demographic behaviour. It has specific implications about the organization of the process of production round the members of the family under the direction of the head of the household. It carries over to the distribution of the product among the producers-members of the family by rules other than marginal productivity considerations. Finally, it makes meaningless the definition of functional shares, since the return to the family's land, labour capital and entrepreneurship are interwoven – and this can have implications both for production and for consumption. It is possible, in short, that the socio-economic organization of the agricultural sector specifies the direction of the intergenerational wealth flow as going from younger to older generations. It is this organization of the agricultural sector, then, more than any specific set of intervening variables, which operates to make fertility rates endogenous to agricultural development /Caldwell 1976/. Unhappily, the evidence connecting the organization of the agricultural sector to demographic characteristics is sparse.   Some of the research in this project relates directly to this evidence.

Agricultural Growth and Fertility Declines

The various attempts to relate demographic variables to agriculture-specific variables have generally been unsuccessful, with the possible exception of rural employment (Table 3.2). Variables describing the structure of development such as the rate of growth in agricultural GDP, the share of agriculture in GDP and agriculture's share in total population, do not seem to contribute to the explanation of declines in fertility.   Similarly, no clear pattern emerges in the relationship between food production and population /Abercrombie 1969, p. 4/. This evidence can be interpreted to mean either that there is no relationship between agricultural development and fertility, and therefore none can be revealed by the data;   or, alternatively, that, while a relationship exists, it cannot be captured by the rate of growth in agricultural GDP - a variable which should be no better an index of development (and is probably a worse one) than the growth in per capita income.

None of these two simple explanations is sufficient, and the problem of discovering economic, social and demographic interrelationships which may exist at the sectoral level becomes complicated by conceptual and methodological considerations and by constraints in data availability.   While development in general may well be related to declines in fertility, it is also reflected in a decrease in the relative size and importance of the agricultural sector.   At a certain level of aggregation, then, it becomes hard to distinguish whether it is a growth or a decline in agriculture which would be associated with declines in fertility. At the household level, on the other hand, the issue may be more clearcut, but for the fact that the relevant household data are not readily available.   Finally, data on sector-specific fertility rates do not exist.   If, on the contrary, one were to associate, changes in agricultural population with agriculture-specific socio-economic variables, the effect of the latter on fertility would have been swamped by migration.   Without having a valid migration model, or sector-specific demographic data including fertility rates, one cannot conduct a rigorous analysis of the demographic-economic interactions at the sectoral level of agriculture.

It is for these reasons that the following analysis will have to be largely restricted at the conceptual level, and, at the empirical level, will rely, at best, on casual quantification.

Agricultural growth sets in motion forces which have multiple and varied implications for social, economic and demographic development. Depending on the form taken by agricultural growth, its effects on fertility may also be several, and they may take time to materialize. It would certainly be an oversimplification if one relied on economic changes incipient in agricultural growth as a means of solving the population problem.

Eva Mueller /1974; 1976/ has studied some celebrated cases of successful and sustained agricultural growth - including those of Japan and the Indian Punjab - with an eye for their implications for declines in birth rates. Her conclusion is that the decrease in birth rates appeared with a substantial lag and was mainly as a result of factors other than the increase in farm incomes. In fact, the first manifestation of agricultural growth in both cases was the release of the income constraint on population growth and an immediate increase in birth rates. The decrease in mortality rates, because of better nutrition and hygiene, occurred first. Rapid rates of increase in agricultural population ensued. The birth rates started to decline, first moderately (in the twenties, for example, in Japan, following the onset of the growth in agriculture with a 50-year lag), and only later on substantially. This occurred in the early fifties in Japan, and in the late sixties in Punjab. There is also micro-economic cross-section evidence concerning the observation that birth rates rise initially with income levels, and only when a "threshold income" is reached do they decline /Encarnación 1974/.

Such observations may be explained away as statistical artifacts. They may be due to "errors in measurement", since education and efficiency of public administration are closely correlated with the level of development and with incomes, and the positive relationship may therefore be due to more complete reporting of births. Furthermore, the persistent increase in birth rates during periods of increasing incomes may merely reflect the age structure of the population resulting from a historical record of high birth rates and the decrease in death rates contemporaneous with development. Evidence on fertility rates during these periods, which would have been the crucial variable, does not exist. Systematic explanations of the positive relationship between income levels and birth rates are also possible. The income constraint on population growth may become binding, e.g., where the poorer farmers tend to avert births, and hence excessive subdivision of land. This hypothesis tends to find support in one of the specific contributions (on Hungary) to this Report.

Fertility Declines in Agriculture: The Demographic Record of Hungary

A longitudinal study of the demographic, social and economic development in Hungary prepared for this Report /ANDORKA 1977/ casts some important light on the relationships between agricultural development and fertility declines. The study covers four distinct historical periods:

(i) The preindustrial, late feudal period (1700-1867).

(ii) The period from 1867 to 1919, i.e., from the political compromise with the Hapsburg Kings to the end of the first world war when Hungary lost more than one half of its land and population. This was the period of the industrial take-off and of the developing capitalist economy.

(iii) The interwar and second world war period of stagnating capitalism.

(iv) The contemporary period of socialist development (1945-75).

The pre-industrial, late feudal period is of particular importance for the identification of some determinants which are probably crucial for fertility declines in the agricultural sector. This period can be divided into two subperiods — on either side of roughly 1787. There are no definite data on fertility for the first subperiod, but the population seems to have doubled between 1720 and 1787. Even if immigration was on an exceptionally large scale, the natural rate of growth of population must have been very high — probably among the highest in Europe — to account for this increase. On the other hand, the rate of population growth declined dramatically in the rest of the period, since the population doubled in approximately 110 years (1787 to 1900).

The social organization of agriculture and the availability of land seem to be important for the explanation of fertility behaviour during these two subperiods. First, the country was predominantly agrarian. An estimated 75 percent of the population earned their living from the land. Second, food production during the period grew slightly more than population, and this was accomplished without an increase in yields. The third characteristic is that the agricultural sector was organized around the seignioral (manorial) system. Landowners formed less than one percent of the population, and the serfs almost 50 percent. The serfs were originally allotted "1 serf-plot" (i.e. a plot sufficient to provide a livelihood for one family), and they had to pay 1/10 of their production to the Catholic Church, 1/9 of the remaining produce to the landlord. They also had to do corvée (forced labour) for the lord to the manor. Serfdom was abolished in Hungary in 1848 when the serfs acquired title to the land worked by them. Another 30 percent of the population were peasant cotters, i.e., agricultural labourers. Fourth, the supply of land changed during this period. In the first part of the 18th century, land was freely available in the previously Turkish-occupied part of the country (in the Great Plain and Southern Transdanubia) which was drastically depopulated during the wars. As a result, the landlords were glad to allot land to serfs willing to cultivate it and pay the taxes. During the latter half of the eighteenth century, land gradually became scarce as population grew, and landlords tried to expand their manorial estates. As a result, "½, 1/4 or 1/8 serf-plots" started appearing in the census.

Family reconstitution studies from parish registers focus on serf households of two marriage cohorts, 1750-1790 and 1791-1850 and help cast light on the demographic development outlined above. First, in village communities, early marriage was customary and celibacy was rare. Second, almost all the households of the smallholder serfs were of the extended and multiple-family type, i.e., parents tended to live together with one or several married children. Third, the early cohort had high fertility rates, while, in the 1791-1850 cohort, a dramatic decline in birth rates as a result of birth control makes its appearance. There was also a decline in mortality, but not a very significant one.

The conclusion is that the preindustrial, late feudal period of 1700-1867 is composed of two subperiods with distinct patterns in fertility behaviour. First, and up to the middle of the 18th century, birth rates were very high. This coincided with the period of ample land supplies in depopulated Southern Transdanubia when the landlords were encouraging immigration, and the sons of peasants could obtain new serf-plots. In these circumstances, the larger families were not at a disadvantage, since they did not need to subdivide the land among the adult children.

The situation changed in the second part of the period. Uncultivated land became scarce. As transport systems improved, the landlords began their own manorial production, which became profitable, and they attempted to reclaim the land which the serfs were cultivating. Furthermore, the serf's access to the woods and pastures was restricted, and this became even more serious after the abolition of serfdom when all common lands or surfaces, including pastures, lakes and rivers, were deeded exclusively to the landlords. If population growth had not been restricted by birth control, the level of living of the serfs would have deteriorated, or population pressure would have had to be relieved, either by having the serfs' sons work as agricultural cotters, or by migration. The former solution was regarded as beneath the social dignity of the serfs, and there were no easy avenues of migration (not least because serfs were mostly Calvinist, and were restricted in their movements by the ban on building a church where there was none before).

As a result, the demographic patterns observed in Hungary during this period were quite different from what the demographic transition theory has described as the "European pattern". (a) While in Europe fertility started to decline in the late 19th century, in Hungary the drop in fertility began much earlier – around 1780. (b) While the distinctive patterns of fertility declines in Europe included delay in marriage and high rates of celibacy /YOTOPOULOS 1977/, in Hungary, the age of marriage was low, celibacy normal, and the emphasis was on birth control in marriage. (c) In Europe, fertility declines coincided with the spread of single family and nuclear family households. It is also the prevalent opinion among demographers that extended family and multiple family households are associated with higher fertility, since they are correlates to lower income levels, and since the presence of grandparents makes it cheaper to raise children. In Hungary, on the contrary, the fertility declines took place within the extended family system, and there is evidence that the parents of the young couples specifically encouraged the practice of birth control.

In the first two decades of the industrial take-off period (1867-1919), fertility in Hungary increased, but then started declining again. The subsequent declines in fertility were more pronounced among the urban white-collar strata, and also among the self-employed peasants, as compared to the industrial workers and the agricultural workers. While it appears that self-employed farmers reacted to recessions and economic hardships by practising birth control, the labourers chose to emigrate to the cities and overseas.

In the interwar period and up to the end of the second world war (1919-45), the self-employed peasants responded to the economic stagnation by further limiting their family, as did the urban workers, especially since the avenues of emigration were now closed to them. The fertility of agricultural workers, on the other hand, especially those who worked on estates, remained high.

The final period of socialist development is characterized, first, by the land reform which gave small plots to the majority of agricultural workers. Soon after, their fertility declined. In the following years of rapid industrialization, labour was drawn from agriculture into industry (although most of those affected still resided on the farms). Furthermore, since the collectivization was completed in 1961, the income levels of members of agricultural cooperatives and of agricultural workers rose to the income levels of industrial workers. Parallel with those developments, the fertility rates of cooperative peasants, of agricultural workers and of non-agricultural workers converged — the latter being only slightly lower than the others.

The following tentative conclusions can be drawn from the demographic experience of Hungary as analysed in this Report:

1. The decline of fertility started much earlier than the take-off to industrialization, i.e. in pre-modern conditions when economic circumstances, such as the scarcity of land, would have led to impoverishment of families with a large number of children and of communities with a rapidly growing population.

2. The take-off to industrialization resulted in an increase in fertility, especially of the industrial workers for varying periods. Economic depressions, however, sooner or later led to a new drop in fertility.

3. Different social strata in peasant societies tend to respond differently to similar economic conditions. Smallholder peasants, who fear impoverishment in consequence of large families, i.e. many inheritants, seem to be more prone to practise birth control in marriage than landless workers.

4. On the other hand, landless workers tend to be more prone to emigrate to foreign countries or to migrate to towns.

5. Land reform, by providing a small farm to the landless workers, rapidly results in the adoption by the new self-employed peasants (ex-workers) of the demographic strategies

of the previously self-employed peasants, i.e., the limitation of the number of children.

6. When the economic and social conditions of those employed in agriculture become similar to the conditions of non-agricultural workers (e.g. as regards wages, working hours, and social insurance), they soon tend to adopt the demographic behaviour of the non-agricultural workers, i.e. their fertility ceases to be higher.

Thus, it would appear that peasants – both in premodern and modern conditions – behave in an economically rational way when they decide to marry and to have children. This means that, when a large number of children endangers their level of living, they tend to reduce their fertility. The correlation is not so unambiguous when incomes are increasing. It seems that it is not so much the absolute level of income as the relative level in terms of the aspirations of the couples which determines the number of children. Aspirations may rise more rapidly than actual income, and in that case couples will tend to reduce their fertility. A more equal income distribution, less unequal chances of social mobility, more equal education and so on tend to contribute to raising aspirations.

Modernization of Agricultural Production, Fertility Declines and Migration

The hypothesis of induced innovation has been advanced by Hayami and Ruttan /1971/ to explain the introduction of chemical-biological agriculture as a result of changes in relative prices. An equivalent hypothesis had been advanced earlier by Boserup /1965/ and Clark /1967/ to describe the process of labour intensification and of land expansion (vertical and horizontal agricultural growth) observed in the past in a number of countries. According to this hypothesis, population growth is the exogenous shock which induces more extensive-agriculture by bringing into cultivation new lands, or more labour-intensive-agriculture by changing the crop-mix in such a way that total output increases without a concomitant decrease in the marginal product of labour. Such agricultural innovations, in turn, make it possible for a country to support a larger population. The agricultural development in Japan, as well as at least part of the agricultural growth in the Punjab and in China fits this model /Mueller 1974, pp. 319 ff./.

The obverse hypothesis has been suggested by Mueller /1974, pp. 320 ff./, based on the cash needs of modern chemical-biological agriculture for the purchase of improved seeds, chemical fertilizers, plant protection materials, tube wells, implements, etc. In this context, the externally produced inputs compete with children in the total allocation of household expenditure, with the result that they exert some downward pressure on fertility.

There are two variants of the "psychological hypothesis" which links agricultural modernization to declines in fertility. One suggests that a successful experience with agricultural innovations, for example, of the Green Revolution variety, will make families prone to experiment in other aspects of life too, such as birth control /Johnston and Kilby 1975, Ch. 4; Brown 1970/. This is a testable, but as yet untested hypothesis. A parallel hypothesis of psychological linkage has been suggested by Epstein /1962/ who views some of the new agricultural practices as disruptive of traditional relations and of social norms, to the extent that they facilitate certain kinds of modern behaviour. In her study of two Indian villages, Epstein found that:

> economic changes which alter the sources of livelihood available to a village (in the case of one of her villages, greater access to non-farm employment in the neighbour-hood) do produce extensive social change and modernization in the village. By contrast, innovations which raise agricultural income without fundamentally altering people's work situation (in the case of her other village, availability of new irrigation facilities) evoke much less change in traditional norms and ways of life. It may well be that the Green Revolution has an influence similar to the introduction of new irrigation facilities /Mueller 1974, p. 324/.

In conclusion, one can say that there is no a priori solid evidence to suggest that the agricultural change introduced through the chemical-biological technology may have any direct effect upon fertility rates in LDCs. To the extent that the Green Revolution has an impact on a specific country, that impact may well be that it buys time in which to solve the population problem.

The contribution to this Report by STARK /1977/ extends the agricultural modernization hypothesis to include rural-to-urban migration. As we noted previously (Chapter II), the need for technological change becomes endogenous through the change in the age composition of the family unit. However, technological change is hindered by the very characteristics of the new technology, i.e., by its requirements for an agricultural surplus to be invested and by its subjective risk-increasing nature. At the same time, the introduction of new technology is subject to a set of internal and external constraints. The absence of fully functioning market structures and of appropriate institutional arrangements (especially credit and insurance schemes) implies that the constraints cannot be alleviated through the highly fragmented markets (because of the prevalence of production risks and aversion

to them and because of the low level of surplus).   The easing of these constraints becomes
a critical condition for carrying out technological change.   This is done through the rural-
to-urban migration of a family member which bypasses the credit and insurance markets, and so
corrects for the bias which the operation of the market introduces against the small farmer.
This migration, then, has a dual role with respect to the agricultural family unit - the
accumulation of surplus to invest in technological change (where migration acts as an intermediate investment, the returns to which are remittances), and the diversification of the
income-creating portfolio of assets.

Nutrition as a Contributing Factor to Agricultural Development

Economists have tried to introduce a nutrition component into the analysis of production through the "wage-productivity relationship".[1]   These attempts have met with little
success, and the main reason for this failure is that the data needed by economists in order
to measure the impact of better nutrition on production are different from those collected
by nutritionists.   A contribution to this Report /BLISS AND STERN 1977/ developed a production and labour market hypothesis incorporating a nutritional component, and proceeded to
examine the evidence on the specific relationship between nutrition and productivity.   We
will present the discussion on that evidence here, since it casts light on the data needed
in order to examine nutrition as a determinant of agricultural development.

The main concerns of nutritionists have been the energy requirements of individuals.[2]
The focus of economists, on the other hand, is the relationship which transforms food calories
into work for an individual of given skill, intelligence, psychology, etc.   This is the
minimum specification of the economists' requirements, and it is the subject of this review.
Undoubtedly, an individual's health, strength and general performance are also affected by
other long-term aspects of higher living standards, as, for example, by better hygiene and
a more balanced diet in proteins and vitamins.   It would seem, however, that it is premature
to review these aspects from the economist's standpoint.

In formulating a functional relationship relating tasks performed to calorific impact,

---

[1] For example see Leibenstein /1957/, Yotopoulos /1965/.

[2] See for example FAO/WHO /1973/, and Durnin and Passmore /1967/.

we draw heavily on a paper by Payne and Dugdale /1975/. When food is absorbed by the body, the available energy may be used in different ways. The individual may perform work, he may put on weight, and he has to maintain the fabric of his body. Assuming constant body temperature, the energy absorbed must be equal (by the first law of thermodynamics) to the sum of the energy involved in these different uses. The determinants of the amount of energy involved in the different uses, and the functional forms associated with these determinants, are matters for both theory and experiment, and will vary across individuals, but the accounting equation remains the same in the sense that we add across the different uses to get the total used. Let the calories absorbed by an individual (net of those excreted from the system) in some period be c. Suppose the weight of the individual is W (in kg). Then we have (assuming constant body temperature)

$$c = \frac{1}{e} f(n,W) + \alpha \Delta W + kW^{\beta} \qquad \text{/1/}$$

The first term on the right hand side of equation /1/, $\frac{1}{e} f(n,W)$, is the energy used up in performing n tasks: the work done is f(n,W) and e is the efficiency of the body in converting energy into work — e being often thought to be around 0.25 /Mountcastle 1968, p. 532/. The work done by the individual in, say, digging would be the raising of soil, overcoming friction in loosening the soil, moving around the field, and so on.

The second term of the equation represents the energy retained by the body in weight increases over the period (so that, for a decrease $\Delta W < 0$). The constant will depend, inter alia, on the form in which the energy is stored; in particular, the proportion stored as fat — to give orders of magnitude however, /Davidson et al. 1975, Ch. 3/, one might expect α to be about 5 000 (5 calories give 1 gm).

The third term represents the maintenance energy required at minimum activity levels merely to maintain the fabric of a body at given weight. This was taken by the FAO/WHO committee /FAO/WHO 1973, p. 37/ as 1.5 x BMR where BMR is the basal metabolic rate, or the energy used (thus, heat produced) under resting and fasting conditions. The extra 50 percent is for the heat generated in the absorption of food, a "minimum" level of voluntary muscular activity, such as dressing and washing, and the synthesis of tissue. This maintenance energy divided by weight in kg to the power 0.75 shows a striking constancy across different animals $\underline{/}$FAO/WHO 1973, p. 3$\underline{7}$, including humans, and seems to give k around 105 cals kg -0.75. The third term is much the most important constituent of daily calorie recommendations. For example, the FAO/WHO $\underline{/}$1973, p. 38$\underline{7}$ report suggests 2 600 calories for maintenance and 400 calories for moderate activity for a 65 kg male, at mean ambient external temperature 10°C, aged 20-39, to give a total of 3 000 calories per day. We shall, following FAO/WHO, call him the reference man.

For expository purposes, we have offered a particular form of the equation in $\underline{/}$1$\underline{7}$. It is important to realize that equation $\underline{/}$1$\underline{7}$ is not, as it stands, the relation which economists are trying to identify. It is a vital first step, however, and we shall discuss the further steps involved in transforming it into the relation between productivity and consumption later, when we examine the implications of the nutritional evidence.

We now turn to the problems of specification and estimation, and take the three terms in $\underline{/}$1$\underline{7}$ in increasing order of difficulty. The issues raised by the second term are relatively straightforward, although both precise and general estimates should not be expected. The value of $\propto$ will depend on the proportion of energy stored as carbohydrate (giving approximately 4 cals/gm), and the proportion as fat (which is approximately 9 cals/gm). This varies across individuals. The value of $\propto$ will be lower for an increase in weight than for a decrease, so that, strictly speaking, our notation $\propto \triangle W$ is illegitimate $\underline{/}$Payne and Dougdale 197$\underline{5}$.

The problems increase when we turn to the third term. Davidson et al. $\underline{/}$1975, p. 3$\underline{7}$ suggests that, across humans, β = 1 seems to do as well as β = 0.73 (the figure given by them across species), and indeed the FAO/WHO committee $\underline{/}$1973, p. 7$\underline{9}$ eventually base their recommendations on β = 1. But, for an individual losing weight, these values of β do not seem appropriate. Payne and Dugdale $\underline{/}$1975, p. 1$\underline{3}$, using data from a semi-starvation experiment, show that β = 2 models the decline for this energy requirement rather well. This number would not necessarily be appropriate for maintenance requirements for given W in the long run, since adaption takes place (see below).

The allowance of 50 percent above BMR in the calculation of maintenance energy at "minimum" activity levels may itself be reduced if food is cut back. It is worth quoting here at length from Davidson et al. $\underline{/}$1975, pp. 39-4$\underline{0}$, since it will also be relevant for our discussion of the first term $\frac{1}{e} f(n,W)$ — the energy expended at work.

When European men in prisoner of war camps in the Far East were given a ration providing only 1600 cals daily, they lost weight at first rapidly, but later slowly (Smith and Woodruff, 1951). After an interval of many weeks and when the body weight had been reduced by 20 to 25 percent the losses ceased and many of them survived till liberation three years later with their body weight stable at this low level. In the Minnesota experiment on volunteers subjected to partial starvation, Keys and his colleagues (1950) showed a similar adaption to a low energy intake with stabilization of body weight at a new lower level. They were able to demonstrate that this adjustment was in part due to a fall in metabolic rates, consequent upon the reduction on cell mass, but the main factor was a marked reduction in voluntary physical activity. Here is an example of the control of body weight by a variation in energy expenditure.

Given that, of the 3 000 cals/day for the FAO/WHO reference man, 400 is for moderate activity over and above "minimum", 1 700 for the BMR and 900 for the 50 percent above BMR (working in round numbers), the natural interpretation of the remarks of Davidson et al. is that one can cut into this 50 percent by a reduction in "minimum" activity.

Let us summarize the position on total recommended energy levels, accepting the FAO/WHO estimate of 400 cals/day for the energy requirements of moderate activity above the minimum. We begin with the FAO/WHO recommendation of 3 000 cals/day for the reference 65 kg man at $10^{\circ}C$ and aged 20-39, and, to give an example of the range of possible disagreement, we calculate a low estimate of the requirement for the reference man to maintain constant body weight performing moderate tasks at $25^{\circ}C$. We have suggested that 160 cals/day could be saved by uniform (non-varying) eating and activity levels. There could be a 200 cals/day reduction for the higher ambient temperature. Further, and this is rather speculative, it may be possible to cut into the 50% above BMR for minimum activity levels by, say, 200 cals/day (over and above the 160 reduction for uniformity). Thus, a low estimate, accepting 400 cals/day for moderate activity and the FAO/WHO estimates of BMR, would be 2 440 cals/day. However, the FAO/WHO say (p. 107) that "a variety of values /of the BMR/ have been reported in the literature". We have not surveyed these values, but we give an example from the internal evidence of FAO/WHO itself. In Table 9 p. 37, they quote from Calloway and Spector /1954/ a maintenance energy intake for an adult man as 34 cals/kg/day. This is to be compared with the 1.5 BMR of the calculation of their recommendations, thus, with $\frac{2\,600}{65} = 40$ cals/kg/day. Now the use of 34 cals/kg/day, instead of 40, would reduce the 2 600 for the reference man to 2 210.

Thus, a systematic choice of the low figure, wherever possible, could reduce the 3 000 by $(160 + 200 + 200 + 390) = 950$ to 2 050 cals/day. We should emphasize that we are **not** suggesting this as a recommendation, and emphasize further the four assumptions different from FAO/WHO which are used in deriving the figure. We merely wish to give an indication of the range of possible disagreement, which seems to us to be very large.

We have been concerned so far in this section to synthesize the nutritional literature on energy and work around equation /1 /. We have ignored certain important topics in order to concentrate on the bare essentials of the equation and to keep the length of the discussion within reasonable bounds. [1]

We will now examine the connection between /1 / and productivity. It is clear from the calorie approach of this section that we must consider the relation as a fairly long-run phenomenon. In the short run, one can perform work without any food intake by reducing body weight, although, of course, for stable body weights on average over time, the energy stored in the body must be replaced.

The energy from ingested food is available fairly quickly. A graph of available energy from food against time from ingestion of food would show a peak after an hour or so, the majority of energy being available within three or four hours /Garrow 1974, pp. 146-147 /. However, unless energy usage is perfectly synchronized with energy availability from the food, there will be storage in, or extraction from, the body. It is this role of the body as a store which implies that the energy relation cannot be a short-run phenomenon.

A body weight which is on the average stable may fluctuate over quite long periods. [2]

---

[1] A more detailed discussion of the nutritional literature can be found on the chapter on energy in Davidson et al. /1975, Ch. 3 /. For an examination of the problems of randomness, see Payne and Dugdale /1975 /, and for measurement of the energy costs of various activities, Durnin and Passmore /1967 /. Further sources of evidence are given in Bliss and Stern /1976 /.

[2] A study of naval cadets (provided with as much food as they wished) showed a daily intake of food closely correlated with activities carried out two days previously /Mountcastle 1968, p. 509 /. Davidson et al. /1975, pp. 38-39 / quote a careful study of a woman who had a weekly cycle losing on average 1 lb per day on week-days and replacing this at weekends. And she was unaware of this cycle until the results were analysed. Haswell /1975 /, in the village studied in Gambia, that there was a yearly cycle in body weight given the agricultural work calendar and availability of food. Given the behaviour of the body as an energy store, we must consider the theory, insofar as it is based on energy rather than psychology, as referring to a period longer than a few day, and frequently much longer.

But what should we assume as regards the long-run weight adjustment? Let us now turn to equation $[1]$ and examine alternative approaches. Since we are taking the long run, we assume that (on average over a few days) ΔW is zero, and thus that weight has settled down to a steady level for given (c, n). Thus, we have

$$c = \frac{1}{e} f(n,W) + kW^{\beta} \qquad\qquad [2]$$

On the other hand, we can abandon the assumption of given weight $\overline{W}$ and go to a different extreme, namely, that, given (c,n), the weight adjusts to a long-run equilibrium value determined by $[2]$. But this would seem to imply no relation at all between (c,n). We could pick any (c,n) pair we wished, and there would be a long run equilibrium W.

Both these specifications are implausible because they ignore the notion of strength or muscle power. We think of a person as being too weak to perform a certain task or more than a certain number of tasks. This idea is best captured in terms of a relation between W(n) which would describe the minimum weight required to achieve a number of tasks n. Indeed many nutritional standards are now measured, as in Gopalan and Vijaya Raghavan $[1969]$, in terms of weight (usually in relation to height) as the most appropriate summary measure of strength. (It is obvious, in this context, that we are not concerned with problems of obesity, and that one should discuss proteins in the building of muscle). The idea of minimum weight W(n) seems important for the theory, and requires further research.

Let us suppose, then, that a W(n) function can be defined. Equation $[2]$ becomes

$$c = \frac{1}{e} f(n,W(n)) + kW(n)^{\beta} \qquad\qquad [3]$$

This is now a relation between c and n, and we take it to be the definition of the relation. We have discussed β and the f(...) function. Thus, in order to determine the shape of the frontier, we still have to discuss W(n). It is clear that the function W(n) will vary across individuals, and will not be easy to define for any one individual, but this function seems indispensable to the relation which we seek. Presumably, W increases with n, and W(0) is positive.

We shall not discuss the W(n) relation further here, but we will draw together some of the lessons from this examination of the nutritional literature. We have concentrated only on energy, and have therefore based our discussion on the first law of thermodynamics as embodied in equation $\underline{/1\underline{/}}$. We saw that the relation between productivity and consumption, if it is to be based on energy, must be considered as long-term since in the short-run the body acts as a store. We saw also that the energy "required" to do tasks is difficult to specify precisely since, when energy input is changed, humans can adapt in the way they perform. The estimates of the energy necessary for maintaining bodily functions with a minimum of work for productive activities vary widely. The relation, if it is to be long-run and based on the first law of thermodynamics, requires the notion of the minimum weight necessary to perform tasks. Furthermore, the level of blood sugar may in some individuals be important in controlling the feeling of fatigue, and the level of blood sugar may, in some individuals, be related to the pattern of food intake.

Our conclusions, then, from the point of view of identifying a relation between nutrition and productivity, are fairly negative. We hope, however, that we have been positive in identifying a method of approach and in pointing to further research requirements. Finally, we should draw attention to the direction of causation implicit in our discussion. We have been supposing that the causation runs from the right hand side of $\underline{/1\underline{/}}$ to the left hand side, and thus, from calories ingested to work capability. The standard labour supply model where the worker chooses the effort which he wishes to supply would portray choice of food consumption and work as determined simultaneously by the individual given prices, incomes and his physical condition.

From Agricultural Growth to Nutrition and Fertility Declines

In the previous section, nutrition was approached as contributing to development through the wage-productivity relationship. In this section, we trace the sequence from growth of agricultural output (and income changes) to improved nutrition, and finally to fertility. In this task, we will review first the sparse evidence on nutrition and fertility $\underline{/}$Huenemann, 1975$\underline{/}$ and next certain relationships between agricultural growth and nutrition as revealed in a study prepared for this Report $\underline{/}$PANIKAR et al.1977$\underline{/}$.

The view that malnutrition stimulates fertility was put forward some time ago $\underline{/}$De Castro 1952$\underline{/}$, but has now been discredited. McNaughton $\underline{/}$1975$\underline{/}$ quotes the findings of a study $\underline{/}$Chávez and Martínez 1973$\underline{/}$ of village women in Mexico in which longer-than-expected amenorrhea after childbirth was observed for the malnourished group, while the group receiving a dietary supplement resumed menstruation earlier. The same positive underlying relationship between nutrition and fertility seems to be strengthened by findings relating the health of the mother to the number of pregnancies /Wishik and Van der Vynckt 1975/. Conversely, repeated and closely spaced pregnancies deplete the maternal stores of calcium and iron, and result in both malnourished mothers and children. An interesting study on pre-school children in Colombia found that, only after births were spaced with at least three years in between, did the incidence of malnutrition drop from 40-50 percent to less than 30 percent /Wray and Aguirre 1969/.

The conclusion from this sketchy review of the literature is that the direct effect of improved nutrition on fertility must be positive. The inclusion of nutrition as an instrument of population policies - as distinct from nutrition as an objective of development - can only rest on the indirect effects that a fall in infant and child mortality could have on the parents' planned target of children. As we have already noted, when parents recognize the increased probability of survival for children, they may not plan for an additional child as replacement, and as a result may achieve lower fertility levels /Taylor 1973/. The question arising is the length of the time lag between the decrease in mortality and the modification of parents' reproductive behaviour. There is some evidence that this lag may be as small as two to three years /Wray 1972; Schultz 1971/.

While the impact of nutrition on fertility declines is rather indirect, there is some evidence in favour of a tentative hypothesis connecting agricultural development - as distinguished from overall income growth - with nutrition. More specifically, evidence from India /United Nations 1975, p. 8 ff./, suggests that calorie intake is more closely related to the level of foodgrain production than to the level of per capita income. It would appear that the variation in per capita calorie intake is much less than the variation in per capita incomes. More important, some poor countries which have a relatively large agricultural sector (in terms of labour force in agriculture) and a high per capita production of foodgrains, appear to have a higher calories intake per capita than countries at higher levels of development but with a less important agricultural sector.

An analysis of cross-sectoral data from Indian states confirms the observations that nutritional levels, as measured by per capita calorie intake, are more closely associated with per capita foodgrain production than with per capita incomes /United Nations 1975, pp. 10-11/.   In Table 4.1, we classify information from .15 states on the basis of the average of state domestic product per capita and of state per capita foodgrain production. The twelve states on the left-hand side of the table had no significant difference in their per capita state domestic product (SDP), which was below the average for all India.   Yet they had substantial differences in calorie intake per capita related to their statistically significant differences in average food production.   The same pattern is repeated for the four states with a per capita state domestic product above the Indian average.

The calorie intake behaviour described above may be related specifically to the operation of the agricultural sector. · One mechanism operates through the levels of food-grain production, via prices, which vary inversely with the quantity of output.   The Kerala study /United Nations 1975, p. 13/ controlled for prices without being able to explain the differences in calorie intake.   The failure of prices to provide an explanation may be the result of trade restrictions and controls which limit their role.   At the international level, import or export prices and quantities may be controlled.   Similarly, the foreign exchange constraint plus price controls may limit calorie intakes when levels of domestic production are low, without a direct impact on prices being allowed.   This is a case of trade inefficiency at the international level.   At the national level, however, free trade usually operates.   The trade inefficiency is then introduced only if the price differentials between grain-surplus and grain-deficit regions are not sufficient to cover the costs of distribution and to provide, on top, sufficient profit margins to allow for the movement of foodgrains warranted by the regional disparities in incomes and production /United Nations 1975, p. 9/.   Such domestic trade inefficiencies may exist in many countries where food prices are controlled.

These cases describe trade inefficiencies which distort the operation of prices, and which can be readily remedied by removing price controls /YOTOPOULOS 1977/.   Another type of inefficiency, which is given much less consideration in economic circles is the inefficiency of exchange.   It is usually overlooked that trade and exchange are not costless. They involve the use of real resources.   Consider the dynamics of population movements as they apply in many contemporary LDCs, with migration from the countryside to the towns –

Table 4.1

Per Capita Calorie Intake, State Domestic Product
and Production of Foodgrains, 15 Indian States

States where per capita production of foodgrains is		States where per capita state domestic product is	
		Below all-India average	Above all-India average
Below all-India average	SDP (Rs)	286.63	450.80
	Production (kg)	146.13	146.80
	Intake (calories)	2 311	2 213
Above All-India average	SDP (Rs)	287.70	451.31
	Production (kg)	218.24	299.34
	Intake (calories)	2 640	2 871

Note: the sub-groups of states are:
Top left: Assam, Bihar, Jammu & Kashmir, Kerala, Karnataka and Tamil Nadu.
Top right: Gujarat, Maharashtra and West Bengal.
Bottom left: Madhya Pradesh, Andhra Pradesh, Orissa, Rajasthan and
Uttar Pradesh.
Bottom right: Punjab (including Haryana).

Source: United Nations /1975/, Department of Economic and Social Affairs, Poverty, Unemployment and Development Policy: A Case Study of Selected Issues with Reference to Kerala. New Work: United Nations (prepared by the Centre for Development Studies, Trivandrum) (ST/ESA/29).

often if only to increase the pool of the unemployed there. Next, real resources must be expended to move grains from the farms (where the people were in the first place) to the towns in order to feed the unemployed. The existence of a real resource cost for this exchange must imply that the same quantity of food would have fed the same people to a fuller extent if ...ey had remained on the farms and if they had produced it for their own consumption. (The usual assumption, of course, is that the movement of labour out of agriculture makes possible the reorganization of farms on a larger scale, with efficiencies of scale in production and a net addition to output and to marketable surplus. This may or may not be correct).

This discussion suggests that calorie intake may be directly related to the volume of agricultural production at the household level, and, to its distribution across household. Given the volume of agricultural output, and the number of agricultural household being fixed, the more equal the distribution of agricultural production across households, the greater the calorie intake per household. This thesis which sees self-sufficiency as providing an explanation of the relationship between calorie intake and food production can also be reformulated in terms of income distribution.[1]

Suppose that income distribution matters with respect to nutrition and, furthermore, controlling for the level of income, the more equal its distribution, the higher the level of nutrition. Furthermore, suppose that, in the agricultural sector, incomes were more equally distributed than in the non-agricultural sector, again controlling for the fact that incomes are generally higher in the latter than in the former. One would then have expected to find higher levels of nutrition in regions with higher food production per capita, on the assumption that these regions also have a relatively larger agricultural sector. If data on distribution were available for the two sectors, the hypothesis would be directly testable. In the absence of such data, the test must be indirect.

Table 4.2 presents state foodgrain production per capita and (separately for rural and urban areas) calorie intakes and per capita incomes (agricultural and non-agricultural) and prices of cereals for 15 Indian states, 1961/62. The discrepancies in incomes and

---

[1] The following paragraphs draw heavily on the United Nations /1975, pp. 16 ff._7 report, although we have supplied our own interpretation of some relationships.

prices between the two sectors are marked, and they are in the direction expected. The calorie intake per capita is consistently higher for rural areas. Furthermore, in Table 4.3 we provide the same classification as in Table 4.1 with respect to per capita _urban_ income and per capita foodgrain production. The noticeable difference between tables 4.1 and 4.3 is that, in the latter but not in the former, per capita calorie intake is correlated with both per capita foodgrain production and per capita urban incomes. This implies that the relationships determining calorie intake per capita is different in the rural and urban sectors.

Both the price and the ability to pay (i.e., the price and the income elasticity of demand) matter when it comes to moving surpluses from producing to consuming areas, or from the rural to the urban sector. The amount of the marketable surplus in the rural areas, on the other hand, is what matters when surpluses are being created to be moved to the urban sectors. The higher the per capita output of foodgrains, the larger the volume of the marketable surplus. Producers of foodgrains are themselves also consumers of foodgrains. While both large and small producers market a share of their output, the latter are often also purchasers of foodgrains. Since small producers have low incomes and thus suffer from a serious income constraint, the net marketed surplus can be expected to increase with the size of the holding. We would therefore expect (a) that, the greater the inequality of distribution in land, the lower will be the average calorie intake of producers ,and (b) that the lower the per capita output of foodgrains, the smaller the volume of marketed surplus. As for incomes, at least in the rural sector, they become relevant for the determination of calorie intake only with respect to the landless population, which is the smaller, the more equal the distribution of land.[1]

---

[1] The report /United Nations 1975, p. 17/ proceeds to construct an additional argument of exchange inefficiency. The movement of marketable surpluses to the urban sector, where both prices and incomes are higher than rural ones, continues to the point at which prices drop to the level where they can no longer cover the costs of production and distribution. Beyond that point, there remain food deficits in the urban sector which are not covered. And, as a result, there remain marketable surpluses in the rural sector which become available to the landless rural population. Rural prices in surplus states therefore tend to be low and to lead to a higher calorie intake even among the landless population, while, in deficit states prices tend to be high and consumption low. This reinforces the relationship between per capita food production and calorie intake discussed earlier.

Table 4.2

Rural-Urban Differences in Per Capita Calorie Intake:
Incomes and Prices of Foodgrains, 15 Indian States, 1961/62

State	Per capita foodgrain production (kg)	Calorie intake per capita per day		Agricultural income per capita (Rs)	Non-agricultural income per capita (Rs)	Price of cereals (Rs per seer)	
		Rural	Urban			Rural	Urban
Andhra Pradesh	211.4	2 184	1 997	198	707	0.51	0.56
Assam	153.0	2 354	2 140	210	1 818	0.52	0.59
Bihar	159.9	2 541	2 330	136	1 137	0.49	0.56
Gujarat	75.9	2 503	2 115	238	841	0.44	0.56
Jammu & Kashmir	173.3	3 033	2 361	222	628	0.39	0.36
Kerala	61.1	1 631	1 554	204	937	0.46	0.57
Madhya Pradesh	287.7	2 910	2 162	198	811	0.39	0.45
Maharashtra	163.3	2 280	1 916	230	681	0.42	0.61
Mysore	174.4	2 758	2 046	222	1 078	0.44	0.54
Orissa	229.9	2 375	2 233	201	593	0.42	0.54
Punjab	310.4	3 076	2 156	313	1 395	0.40	0.50
Rahasthan	277.1	3 147	2 469	203	999	0.34	0.47
Tamil Nadu	169.2	2 147	1 934	208	601	0.52	0.61
Uttar Pradesh	190.0	2 854	2 162	233	736	0.40	0.45
West Bengal	150.4	2 175	2 040	229	1 193	0.58	0.61

Source: United Nations /1975/, Department of Economic and Social Affairs, Poverty, Unemployment and Development Policy: A Case Study of Selected Issues with Reference to Kerala. New York: United Nations (prepared by the Centre for Development Studies, Trivandrum) (ST/ESA/29).

Table 4.3

Per Capita Total Calorie Intake and Calories from Cereals
and Cereal Substitutes, 15 Indian States: Urban Sector, 1961/62

Per capita urban income / Per capita foodgrain production	Below all-India urban average (Calories)		Above all-India urban average (Calories)	
	Cereals	Total	Cereals	Total
Below all-India average	1 337	1 975	1 478	2 040
Above all-India average	1 515	2 118	1 563	2 297

Notes: The averages of states are classified according to levels of income and production of foodgrains.

The grouping of the states for this table is as follows:

Top left: Gujarat, Jammu and Kashmir, Maharashtra, Tamil Nadu.
Top right: Assam, Bihar, Kerala, Karnataka and West Bengal.
Bottom left: Andhra Pradesh, Madhya Pradesh, Orissa and Uttar Pradesh.
Bottom right: Punjab (including Haryana) and Rajasthan.

Source: United Nations /1975/, Department of Economic and Social Affairs, Poverty, Unemployment and Development Policy: A Case Study of Selected Issues with Reference to Kerala. New York: United Nations (prepared by the Centre For Development Studies, Trivandrum) (ST/ESA/29).

This hypothesis finds confirmation in regression results estimated for the rural sector of 15 states of India /United Nations 1975, p. 18/. The basic results are as follows. (The numbers in paretheses are standard errors):

Total calorie intake per capita =

4 216.44 (616.07)	constant
−0.61 (1.53)	per capita agricultural income
−580.09 (150.37)	coefficient of variation in land distribution
−23.96 (9.23)	price of cerea

$$+2.37 \quad \text{production of foodgrains per capita}$$
$$(0.72)$$
$$R^2 = 0.86$$

From these results, it emerges that 86 percent of the inter-state variation in total calorie intake per capita is explained by the variables in the equation. Furthermore, the statistically significant variables are the production of foodgrains per capita, with a positive coefficient, and the inequality in the distribution of land and in the price of cereals, both with negative coefficients. The coefficient of per capita agricultural income is surprisingly negative, but the variable is not statistically significant.

The conclusion of this discussion on the strength of the data from Kerala is that it may not be sufficient to combat undernutrition by raising the levels of income. In order to raise the standards of consumption, we must also both increase the output of food and reduce inequities in the distribution of land.

An Interpretation of the Economic-Demographic Record of Kerala

Since a United Nations-sponsored study by the Centre for Development Studies, Trivandrum, Kerala, appeared /United Nations 1975/, demographic developments in the Indian State of Kerala have attracted great attention. In this context, the project sponsored a follow-up study by researchers in the Centre for Development Studies /PANIKAR et al. 1977/ in order to extract any further lessons to be learnt on economic-demographic interactions.

Tables 4.4 to 4.7 present a summary of the demographic history of Kerala as reconstituted in the study. It appears from Table 4.4 that, unlike other parts of India, Kerala registered a comparatively high rate of population growth right from the turn of this century. These high rates of population growth were made possible because the death rates started to decline sharply at an earlier date in Kerala than in the rest of the country (Table 4.5). This lower mortality trend is still visible. As of 1972, the crude death rate in Kerala was 9.2 per 1 000 as compared to an India average of 16.09. The crucial factors in the decline of mortality were the programme of public health and sanitation which was initiated at an early stage in the State and contributed to the control of infectious desease, and also the medical care delivery system, which resulted in free medical aid to all, irrespective of the capacity to pay, and which was supported by the wide and even regional location of hospitals and dispensaries. The falls in mortality were followed in recent years by a decline in birth rates (the birth rate in the rural sector dropped from 37 per 1 000 in 1950 to 28 per 1 000 in 1975 (Table 4.6)), and by an even more pronounced decline in fertility rates. The general and total fertility rates were, respectively, 172 and 5.1 in 1959; they declined to 108 and 3.4 in 1975.

Table 4.4

Inter-Censal Rates of Population Increase in Kerala and India, 1901/1971

(percent)

Period	Kerala	India
1901/1911	11.75	5.73
1911/21	9.16	-0.31
1921/31	21.85	11.01
1931/41	16.04	14.22
1941/51	24.76	13.31
1951/61	24.76	21.50
1961/71	25.89	24.50

Source: P.G.K. Panikar et al. /1977/ Population Growth and Agricultural Development: A Case Study of Kerala. Trivandrum: Centre for Development Studies, (mimeo) p. 2.

Table 4.5

Crude Death Rate: Kerala, 1901-1960

Decade	Based on vital statistics	Based on census data
1901-1910	18.6	
1911-20	20.1	
1921-30	14.5	
1931-40	14.7	25.0
1941-50	12.7	20.0
1951-60		16.1

Source: P.G.K. Panikar et al. /1977/ Population Growth and Agricultural Development: A Case Study of Kerala. Trivandrum: Centre for Development Studies, (mimeo) p. 4.

Table 4.6

Birth Rates in Kerala, 1931-75

Period/year (1)	Inter-censal estimates (Kerala) (2)	Sample registration system estimates rural sector (3)
1931-40	40.0	-
1941-50	39.8	-
1951-60	38.9	-
1958-59	-	-
1963-64	-	-
1963-64	-	-
1966	-	37.4
1967	-	36.3
1968	-	33.2
1969	-	31.2
1970	-	31.9
1971	-	31.3
1972	-	31.5
1973	-	29.9
1973-74	-	-
1974	-	26.9
1975	-	28.1

Source: P.G.K. Panikar et al. /1977/ Population Growth and Agricultural Development: A Case Study of Kerala. Trivandrum: Centre for Development Studies, (mimeo) p. 97.

Table 4.7

Average Size of Household, Income and Consumption: Agricultural
Labour Households, Kerala and all India 1964/65

Agricultural labour households	Average household size	Per capita income (Rs per annum)	Per capita consumption (Rs per annum)
Kerala:			
with land	5.78	158	179
without land	5.01	164	169
All India:			
with land	5.00	135	236
without land	4.16	156	208

Source: P.G.K. Panikar et al. /1977/ Population Growth and Agricultural
Development: A Case Study of Kerala.   Trivandrum: Centre for
Development Studies, (mimeo) p. 76.

A number of questions are investigated in the study with respect to this demographic
record in Kerala:

(1) To what extent are these developments in Kerala consistent with current thinking
on the process of the demographic transition?

(2) How did the economy adjust to the record of population growth?

(3) What were the components of the fertility declines?

The Demographic Transition in Kerala and the
Adjustments to Population Pressure

The record of Kerala confirms the observation derived from the demographic analysis
of Hungary above that the demographic transition preceded the take-off to industrialization
or the onset of sustained economic growth.   Indeed, in terms of per capita income, Kerala
is one of the poorer Indian states.   Yet its distribution of income is more equal
(especially if one also considers in-kind income, such as health and education services),
and its literacy rate, particularly for women, is the highest in the country.

This finding was already familiar from the United Nations /1975/ study cited above.
A new issue explored in the current study refers to the social and economic adjustments to

high population growth.   Although the most densely populated state of India, and also one of the poorest, Kerala never suffered from a famine in living memory.   A number of mechanisms explain this fact.

First, cultivation expanded at the extensive margin.   Unlike the valley lands which were suitable for the cultivation of rice and other foodcrops, the marginal lands brought into cultivation were in the valley ridges or the hills, and were suitable for the cultivation of commercial crops, such as coconut, pepper, ginger and turmeric, which had good export markets and fetched attractive prices.   Furthermore, at even higher altitudes, small "garden-plots" were cultivated intensely with tapioca, root crops (yams and colocassia) and fruit crops (bananas and jackfruit).   Within this cropping mix, the output of rice did not keep pace with the growing population, thus creating a gap in the basic staple which was filled through substantial imports of rice.   These inputs were financed through the surplus made possible by the growing cultivation of export commercial crops and the favourable terms of trade.   In periods of worsening terms of trade, however (e.g. from 1916 to 1924) and during abnormal circumstances (e.g. periods of war), when the free inflow of rice was interrupted, there were attempts to increase domestic production of foodcrops through land reclamation, shortening the fallow period, more intensive cultivation and intercropping. However, the most important factor in closing the food gap and maintaining nutrition in Kerala at adequate levels was the switch to inferior staple-substitutes, especially tapioca. This substitution was induced by the price trends in rice and tapioca.   Since 1959, to give one example, the price of rice has roughly tripled (and, in some years such as 1974, even quadrupled).   The price of tapioca also almost tripled.   Tapioca, however, had an advantage of more than 200 percent over rice in terms of calorie yield per hectare of land or per rupee of consumer expenditure.   Moreover, the supply of land suitable for cultivation of tapioca was more elastic than that of rice lands.   As a result, tapioca (supplemented by yams, colocassia, plantains, bananas and jackfruit) provided the basic means of avoiding famine in Kerala.

The second adjustment mechanism at work operated through changes in the distribution of land over time.   High rates of population growth and substantial increase in the man-land ratio, along with lack of rapid economic growth, would be expected to produce serious unemployment and depressed wage levels.   These tendencies were largely kept in check, and real wage levels have even increased.   This happened mainly because (as the spotty data derived mostly from the sixties suggest) the concentration of land declined and the proportion of households cultivating small-holdings increased. (Some 67 percent of the households cultivated up to one acre in 1971, and 95 percent up to five acres.)   Very intense cultivation is practised in these small family plots, and Kerala has the highest index among Indian states of both net output per acre and net output per worker.   Two further characteristics associated with these small family holdings are worth noting. First, small-holdings do not produce exclusively food crops for home consumption, as might have been expected, but are actively involved also in the production of commercial crops. Second, as compared to landless households (Table 4.5), landed households have more members, on the average, lower per capita incomes and higher per capita consumption.   This last characteristic will be discussed in more detail in the following section on the agriculture-specific demographic relations.

The third adjustment mechanism to high population pressure refers to migration.   It is traditionally held that people from Kerala are highly migratory, and that it was mostly the stimulus of poverty which has driven them into every corner of India and every other country in Asia.   The fact is that, until 1931, the state was on balance a net in-migration state, and in 1971 it occupied only fourth place among Indian states in terms of total out-migrants as a percentage of population.   The reason for the popular misconception is that people from Kerala are highly visible migrants, since they occupy a higher proportion of administrative and white-collar jobs in comparison to migrants from other states.   The high quality of migration from Kerala is a correlate of the state's educational level. Another correlate of the quality of migration is the fact that a larger number of households are reporting as having received remittances, and that the average remittance per household is the second highest of any Indian state.

In review, we can state that the adjustments to rapid population growth observed in Kerala are consistent with the agricultural intensification hypothesis mentioned earlier. Although the data were not suitable to test specifically the migration-intensification hypothesis, it is clear that migration did not necessarily serve as a safety valve for population pressure, although, through remittances, it must have contributed to the improvement of nutrition.

The Composition of Fertility Declines in Kerala

Table 4.8 gives the change in the birth rate in Kerala for two periods, 1959/1971 and 1971/1974. The declines in the birth rate are analysed in three component parts.

The first is the sex-age composition of the population. We have already noted in Chapter II that this component of the birth rate is mechanical, and, as a result of the high growth rate of the population in previous years, is of necessity positive. No significance can be attached to this component from the point of view of economic-demographic interactions. It merely serves to remind policy-makers that population programmes, examined intertemporally, must be discounted with a high rate of interest, since every year's delay makes the problem correspondingly more difficult.[1]

In the earlier period 1959/1971, the nuptiality component contributed the largest share in fertility declines. The delay in marriage was especially marked in the age-groups of women of 15 to 24. The number of married women in that group was 30 percent in Kerala in 1969, as compared to 60 percent in all other states. This trend in Kerala is readily explicable, since the average age of effective marriage has been shown to be an increasing function of the level of education.

The factor which acquired special importance in the later period 1971/74 is the decrease in marital fertility. This decrease depends on the availability of birth control facilities and on the willingness of couples to practise birth control. There has been a steady increase in the use of fertility control in Kerala. While, in 1964, only 2.26 percent of the number of eligible couples were practising some form of control (including sterilization) the number rose to 17.7 percent by 1971, and to 30 percent by 1976. This dramatic increase could provide very important insights into the socio-economic antecendents of population growth – but, unhappily, Indian data are not such as to permit a valid

---

[1] The President of the World Bank has estimated that, for every decade of delay in achieving a net reproduction rate of 1.0 (i.e. replacement level), the world's ultimate steady-state population will be about 15% higher. For example, the 1975 Indian population of 620 million will reach a steady-state at the level of 1400 million if net reproduction rate of 1.0 is achieved in year 2000, while it will be at a steady-state of 2000 million people if the replacement level of 1.0 is delayed to year 2020 /McNamara 1977, pp. 10-11/.

investigation. More specifically, we discover that in the couples protected in 1976, over 90 percent of the males had undergone sterilization. This suggests that the decline in fertility is not mainly due to the usual social or economic motivations, a suspicion which is strengthened if we examine in detail the age, family size and socio-economic characteristics of the groups displaying the most significant marital fertility declines during this period.

Table 4.8

Decomposition of Changes in Crude Birth Rate in Kerala
(Percentage changes over indicated periods)

Period covered	Crude birth rate	Changes in crude birth rates due to changes in		
		Sex-age	Nuptia-lity	Marital Fertility
1959/71	-13.5	+ 1.5	- 9.1	- 3.5
1971/74	-15.5	+ 3.6	- 4.1	-15.2

Source: P.G.K. Panikar et al. /1977/ Population Growth and Agricultural Development: A Case Study of Kerala. Trivandrum: Centre for Development Studies, (mimeo)p. 103.

Are There Agriculture-Specific Demographic Relations?

In this chapter, the focus for the study of economic-demographic interactions is the agricultural sector. The size and importance of that sector is one of the reasons for this specific referencing of demographic analysis. In the typical LDC, most population growth takes place in it. As a result, demographic variables influence the growth and structure of the agricultural sector, including employment, output and productivity. In this perspective, demography is an exogenous variable which interacts with agriculture, and the analysis becomes a special case of the discussion in Chapter III.

This chapter was devoted to the indirect mechanisms relating agriculture to population growth by emphasizing specifically the ways in which demographic variables become endogenously determined in the operation of the agricultural sector. Agriculture has been singled out in the literature as the sector exhibiting special demographic behaviour. The reason for the pattern characterizing fertility rates in agricultural households may simply be that certain intervening variables, say traditionalism, education, etc. are agricultural correlates. Exclusively, on this account the discussion of economic-demographic interactions in

Chapter III would also have covered the agricultural sector. It is suggested, however, in this chapter that the causal ordering going from agriculture to demography extends beyond the existence of agriculture-specific values of intervening variables. Agriculture is organized around a corporate, family-based way of life in which the agricultural households constitute farm-firm complexes combining both production and consumption decisions. Within this institutional framework, there is a definite intergenerational wealth flow. It is this characteristic of the sector which is probably at the basis of the distinct fertility behaviour observed for agricultural households.

This special feature of the agricultural sector assumes unique operational significance for the study of economic-demographic interactions. We have already emphasized that the conventional treatment of the topic has suffered from the use of partial approaches which have considered the one set of variables - be they demographic or economic - as exogenous, while analysing their impact on the other set. The proper approach, however, would be to consider both sets of variables as interdependent and determined within a general framework. This can be best done by studying these interrelations within the micro-economics of the agricultural household which combines both production and consumption decisions. Unhappily, such an integration of the two sides of the agricultural household for the study of economic-demographic interactions has not been attempted in the literature.

We have examined in this chapter the impact of agriculture-specific variables on fertility declines, and we have found it rather weak. This is not because agriculture does not matter when it comes to population control. In fact, the reason is exactly the opposite. The agricultural sector, by its sheer size in most LDCs, characterizes the whole pattern and structure of development. The general impact of development on fertility declines - and conversely - examined in the previous chapters is fully applicable to agricultural development as well.

The strongest case which we have been able to make in this chapter for agriculture-specific variables is that of self-sufficiency in nutrition. We have approached food self-sufficiency from aggregate data by considering an index of land distribution along with the other explanatory variables in the relation describing per capita calorie intake. It remains to examine self-sufficiency with micro-analytic data and to do so also at the national level.

The discussion of food self-sufficiency at the agricultural household level brings out the importance of income distribution for demographic policies - although from a partial, sectoral point of view. The implication is that, the greater the extent to which agricultural population participates in development, the greater and the earlier the probable decline in fertility. This hypothesis is consistent with the overall importance of income distribution on fertility discussed earlier. The hypothesis of income distribution , however, has not been tested rigorously for the agricultural sector, although some casual evidence has been accumulated /Kocher 1973, Rich 1973/.

CHAPTER V

GLOBAL MODELLING OF ECONOMIC-DEMOGRAPHIC INTERACTION

The debate on the population-development relationships has led to the production of a number of simulation models of economic-demographic interaction. The main characteristic of such models is that they comprise socio-economic and demographic components which describe the functioning of the respective systems in more or less detail. The two systems are welded together through a number of feedback loops so that, in principle, both consequences and determinants of population growth and of other dimensions of demographic change are accounted for in the solution.

Even before the advent of the economic-demographic models, model builders concerned only with the socio-economic system were accounting in more or less detail for the "consequences" aspect of demographic change via the use in their models of demographic variables (total population, labour force, etc.).

The novelty introduced by economic-demographic modelling, therefore, is to be found principally in the attempt to account for the determinants of demographic change. To a lesser extent, they also contribute to a better handling of the consequences side through the use of more disaggregated demographic information generated by the demographic component of the model.

In this respect, a good rule of thumb for assessing the validity of any particular model for analysing issues of economic-demographic interaction is to examine the few equations representing the feedback loops, viz. the fertility and mortality functions and, when appropriate, the functions of migration, labour force participation, nuptiality and household formation. If such functions suffer from poor formulation/specification and/or they are nearly impossible to estimate for lack of appropriate data, we are left with a model of the socio-economic system which uses exogenous demographic variables generated by the accompanying demographic data generator. Ceteris paribus, there is no compelling reason for preferring this particular socio-economic model to any other one of the larger set of models not belonging to the economic-demographic interaction family.

In the discussion of economic-demographic interaction models, e.g. Arthur and McNicoll /1975/, Quinn /1977/, SANDERSON /1977/, arguments concerning the pros and cons of large models in general, and systems simulation models in particular, tend to be confused with those concerning the particular feature which sets such models apart from others, namely the inclusion of economic-demographic interaction. From this last standpoint, the criteria for evaluating models will vary with the intended utilization of the model. If the objective is, for example, to obtain an answer to the question of whether population growth contributes to or retards growth in per capita incomes in a particular situation or country, it is enough to observe a few core equations of the model in order to see whether a valid answer can be obtained. In many models it will be found that the answer does not depend on the particular situation/country, but it is predetermined in the model because of the functional form used for these core equations /Arthur and McNicoll 1975/. However, planners may be interested in more practical questions of economic-demographic interaction such as the impact of fertility on the labour force participation rates of women or the possibility of influencing internal migration through socio-economic policies. In such cases, some models will be found to be more helpful than others, even though all may share certain defects when it comes to tackling questions such as the one mentioned above.

A Systems Simulation Model for Long-term Population and Economic Planning (PT2 Model) 1/

As mentioned in Chapter I, the project whose activities are reported here included an attempt to look at economic-demographic interaction in the context of formal modelling. For this purpose, a systems model was developed in order to simulate population dynamics, economic change and economic-demographic interaction over the long term, with special emphasis on the agricultural sector /MARTOS 1977/. The intention was to provide a simple analytical tool, which was not too much demanding as regards data, for possible use in long-term planning in situations of demographic change believed to be closely associated with socio-economic development.

1/ The PT2 model is a revised version of the earlier prototype model (PT1). The latter is also known in the literature as the FAO or FAO/UNFPA Model or LTSM Model.

Since we are referring to the model as a possible planning aid, we need to be clear about what kind of planning uses were visualized by the model builder. In the short and medium term, the meaning of the term planning is clearer than in the long-term. In the short and medium-term, planning is a tool of economic decision-making, or in a broader sense economic policy-making. In the case of long-term planning (15-25 years), the interpretation is less direct. Long-term plans seldom serve economic policy directly and actual decisions can hardly be based solely or predominantly, on long-term considerations. Long-term plans, however, have an important dual role in the planning process. Firstly, they provide a basis, a point of departure, from which medium and short-term planning starts. Secondly, they make it possible for short and medium-term plans to be prepared and evaluated, taking into account long-term effects as well.

This conception of the possible planning uses, together with data and resource limitations, has led the model-builder to select only a limited number of issues of long-term relevance to most developing countries around which to build a prototype model. Moreover, the model treats these issues in a simplified manner in recognition of the insurmountable obstacles presented by data paucity and limitations of computational resources in most developing countries.

The choice of systems simulation as the method of model formulation and solution also reflects the model builder's desire to provide a tool which is computationally flexible and easily adaptable to different situations. (A computer package is provided with the model.) It also reflects his conception of policy-making as a process based on a non-rigorous evaluation of various alternatives on the basis of multiple criteria, rather than on the search of optimal values of a single development indicator /MARTOS 1977/.

Like all models of this nature, this model has two basic components -- a demographic one and an economic one. The kind of interaction between the two components depicted in the model is as follows. In the demographic component, fertility and mortality rates are translated into changes in the population size and in its age and sex structures. These variables influence consumption levels in the economic component and, through them, other economic variables, especially investment and indirectly employment, as well as expenditures on education and health. In their turn, consumption, job opportunities and education and health influence fertility and mortality.

It will be seen that the conception of economic-demographic interaction depicted in the model is a fairly conventional one. Population growth increases consumption and affects adversely the growth of investment and hence economic growth, since the model recognizes investment alone as making for economic growth. Lagging economic growth in turn adversely affects the growth of employment and of education and health services, thus reducing their impact on fertility and hence on population growth.

It is obvious that, for countries starting with high population growth and low investment rates, the situation depicted by the model may represent a trap of quasi-stagnation or decline. To set in motion the mechanism of endogenous fertility declines (and thus eventually increasing domestic investment rates) would require a combination of policies involving foreign investment (which is not constrained in the model) and resource allocation to favour labour-intensive sectors, education and health. In addition, the model recognizes the possibility of "autonomous" fertility declines due to "population policies" (e.g. family planning programmes). Such policies, however, are not shown in the economic part of the model as giving rise to resource commitments.

In what follows we shall present a brief verbal description of the main features of the model. A formal statement of the model in equations (71 equations excluding the population data generator component) can be found in the report on the model /MARTOS 1977/.

In the _economic_ part of the model, eight sectors are distinguished. The criteria used in the prototype are the nature of the product and the use in the sector or subsector of family labour (traditional sectors) or hired labour (modern sectors). The criteria for distinguishing sectors are very flexible, and the adaptation of the prototype can use alternative criteria to suit particular socio-economic situations in the different countries. Of the eight sectors, six are non-agricultural (Modern Industry, Traditional Industry, Capital Goods Industry, Construction, Traditional Services and Modern Services - the latter including government) and two are agricultural (Modern and Traditional Agriculture).

For the _non-agricultural sectors_, investment is allocated by policy decision - (total investment, however, is determined endogenously - see below). The sectors produce outputs on the basis of simple Harrod-Domar type production functions. Investment allocations to the two <u>agricultural sectors</u> are likewise policy determined, and so is the distribution of agricultural investment between land expansion and investment on land already under cultivation (intensive investment).   Agricultural production in each of the two sectors is then determined as the product of land area times yield.   For each time period, the former is made up of the land area in the previous period plus additions following the allocation of land-augmenting investment, minus land withdrawn from agricultural use because of construction sector activities.   (An equation in the model makes land withdrawal a function of the construction sector's output.)   Yield is likewise equal to the previous period's level plus two increments: one due to intensive investment allocations and one due to the increased use of current inputs, which change as a function of changes in agricultural GDP in the previous period.

The two previous paragraphs give a complete description of the <u>production mechanism</u> of the model.   It will be seen that labour is not shown as playing any role in production, and this reflects the basic premises of the model builder that "surplus labour" conditions prevail in the typical developing country.   Subsequently, the products of the eight sectors are added together and transformed into total GDP at market prices.   The next set of equations referring to the total economy distribute this total GDP into the conventional expenditure categories of the national accounting system, according to the following rules:

<u>Private Consumption</u> (C_p) is estimated as the product of C_p per capita times population in adult consumer equivalents.   (Hence there is some influence of the age and sex structure on consumption.) C_p per capita grows only if GDP per capita has grown by allocating exogenously, as a matter of policy, a fraction of the increment of per capita GDP to consumption.   If per capita GDP has not grown or has fallen, per capita C_p remains unchanged at the level of the previous period.   Subject to this latter constraint, the model makes the distribution of increments in per capita GDP between savings and consumption a major policy variable, and assumes that the government has sufficient power to impose it.   However, the model does not specify the policy instruments to be used for this purpose.

<u>Government Consumption</u> is assumed to grow at rates determined by recurrent expenditure requirements caused by investment in the government services sector.

<u>Exports</u> are estimated as the sum total of exports of the four sectors assumed to

produce exportables (Modern and Traditional Agriculture and Modern and Traditional Industry).
The share of the output of each sector to be exported is assumed to be a policy variable.
In an alternative version of the model, net foreign borrowing is policy-constrained.   In
this latter case, total exports are determined as residual between total imports and
"permitted" net foreign borrowing.

Imports distinguish between imports of capital goods, of intermediate goods and of
final consumer goods.   Capital goods imports are the difference between the total demand
for capital goods (determined on the basis of the equipment component of total investment
in each sector) and the gross output of the capital goods sector.   Imports of intermediates
are the sum total of such imports into each sector, determined on the basis of import
component coefficients specific to each sector.   Consumer goods imports are the sum total
of the import components of private consumption and government consumption.

Total Gross Investment is derived as a residual from the GDP identity.   Subsequently,
the total gross investment in period t is distributed to the sectors on the basis of policy-
determined proportions.   The resulting sectoral investment allocations are then entered
into the production functions of the sectors, and the process for solving for period t+1
starts all over again.

A constraint is imposed on the solution that total demand for construction output
(a good not entering into international trade) should be approximately equal to the output
of the construction sector as given by the appropriate sectoral production function.   Demand
is determined on the basis of sector-specific coefficients of the construction component in
each sectoral investment allocation.   If an imbalance between supply and demand of construction output is revealed, the initial investment allocation to the construction sector is
revised at the expense (or to the benefit) of investment in other sectors until an appro-
ximate balance is established.

An additional computational routine is included to provide indications of development
in the food situation.   Domestic food demand in aggregate value terms is estimated on the
basis of growth of per capita consumption expenditure, an income elasticity of food demand
and the growth of total population in adult consumer equivalents.   Exports of food are a
proportion of agricultural exports.   Domestic food production is assumed to grow pari passu

with total agricultural output.   The resulting food import requirements are then viewed as an important indicator useful for policy-making.   The model makes no provision, however, for feedback effects to other economic variables and relations.

A separate component of the model is devoted to the simulation of the effects of the developments traced in the economy on the distribution of labour to the different sectors and the employment/unemployment implications for the modern sectors only.

Firstly, the total labour force is estimated by applying exogenous sex and age-specific labour force participation rates to the total population resulting from the demographic submodel.   Subsequently, the total labour force is distributed among two groups: the labour supply to the group of modern sectors (Modern Agriculture, Modern Industry, Modern Services, Capital Goods Industry, and Construction) and the labour supply to the group of traditional sectors (Traditional Agriculture, Traditional Industry and Traditional Services).

The division of the total labour supply into its two components is made in the following manner.   The labour supply in the group of modern sectors increases at the growth rate of the total population of working age, and in addition receives a transfer of labour from the group of the traditional sectors.

The rate of labour transfers in period t is a function of the growth rate of labour supply in the traditional sectors in period t-1 and the productivity differential (income per member of the labour force) in the two groups of sectors.   Moreover, the rate of labour transfer is also influenced by developments in the relative shares in the two groups of sectors in total labour supply.   If such shares tend to move apart from each other, a gravity-multiplier slows down the process of labour transfer, while it reinforces the transfer when the two shares move towards a 50-50 situation.   This is meant to reflect the idea that, ceteris paribus, the propensity to migrate (labour transfer) tends to increase at the initial stages of urbanization and slows down at a more mature stage, here arbitrarily taken to be reached when the urban (modern) sector attains a share of 50 percent /Wéry et al. 1974/.

Once we have determined the labour supply to the group of modern sectors, the labour in the traditional sectors is derived as a residual.   The model does not provide for further investigation into what happens to labour in the traditional sectors, particularly as regards the employment situation.   The implicit assumption is that this part of the labour supply is somehow "absorbed" into traditional activities, though there is no implication that absorption is equivalent to productive employment.

Employment and unemployment are, however, determined for the group of modern sectors. For each of the four non-agricultural modern sectors, employment grows as a function of investment on the basis of sector-specific coefficients indicating jobs created per unit of investment.   A separate equation makes these coefficients functions of the unemployment rate whereby their value declines gradually with a declining unemployment rate (indicating the adoption of more capital-intensive techniques as unemployment falls), but it does not rise in the opposite case.

For Modern Agriculture, employment is postulated to grow at the same rate as cultivated land.   Moreover, the increased use of modern inputs and intensive investment also contribute to employment.   The contribution of the latter can be negative if it is thought to be of the labour-displacing type.   The model treats <u>rural-urban migration</u> in a manner entirely analogous to the one used for labour transfers.

As noted at the beginning of this section, the effects of economic variables on demography are depicted in the model with the aid of two functions - a <u>fertility function</u> and a <u>life expectancy one</u>.   The former is of the general form

$$\Delta F = f(E, W, P)$$

where ΔF is the rate of change in the general fertility rate, E is the adult literacy rate which in turn is a function of investment in education, W is an index of modern sector job opportunities for women and P is an index of effectiveness of population policies.   The life-expectancy function is of the general form

$$\Delta L = f(G_o, I_g)$$

where ΔL is the rate of change in life expectancy at birth, G_c is the rate of growth of per capita private consumption expenditure and I_g is the per capita investment in government services.

The above presentation was limited to a matter-of-fact statement of what the prototype

model is.   This presentation, however, is no substitute for reading the full report
/MARTOS 1977/ where the model is presented in a formal manner and where the author discusses
the particular choices made by him.   Critical evaluations are available in SANDERSON /1977/,
FAO /1975a/ and Meadows and Robinson /1977/.   For our part, we feel that, for an agriculture-centred model with emphasis on demographic-economic interaction, the agricultural
sector is treated too summarily, while the links between economy and demography are crude
at best.

The underlying idea that population growth is an unmitigated deterrent to the economic
development of the LDCs is not likely to be applicable without qualification.   The absence
of any effects of population growth on agriculture, particularly traditional agriculture,
is another glaring omission.   The crudity of the fertility function is perhaps unavoidable,
given the paucity of empirical evidence concerning the behavioural correlates of fertility.
However, in an agriculture-centred model, food and nutrition should be shown as influencing
life-expectancy.

In the agricultural submodel, demand plays no role in long-term developments, nor,
for that matter, are relative prices.   Agricultural employment cannot be meaningfully
investigated outside the context of changing crop mixes.   This would suggest the need for
a breakdown of the sector into a small number of subsectors.   The assumption that traditional agriculture changes only in response to government decisions influencing investment
allocations looks rather remote from reality.   Demographic developments in rural areas
are a more likely moving force.   Their consideration would have given the opportunity
for the model to incorporate some agriculture-specific form of economic-demographic
interaction.

Again, the processes of change in modern and traditional agriculture are made
independent of each other, except, of course, that they both draw on a common investment
fund.   This is perhaps legitimate if the modern/traditional distinction is based on the
hired labour/family labour criterion.   However, from a technological standpoint, the
modern sector is likely to expand through a process of technological transformation of
part of the traditional sector.   Finally, the assumption used in the model that land
newly brought under cultivation is as productive as land already under cultivation (yields

are put at the same level) may be the exception rather than the rule, since better land can be expected to be taken up for cultivation first.

A number of the above criticisms have been taken into account in <u>adaptations of the model for application to Pakistan</u> /FAO 1976/ and Egypt /El-Issawy and El-Shafei 1977/. The main modification brought about in the case of <u>Pakistan</u> refers to the breakdown of agriculture into four subsectors along technological and institutional criteria, notably small and large farms and irrigated and rainfed land. The pairwise combinations of these two criteria yield the four agricultural subsectors which are not independent of each other in the modified model.

In the case of <u>Egypt</u>, the main modification refers to the introduction of labour as a factor of production through the introduction of Cobb-Douglas production functions in almost all sectors. Four agricultural subsectors are distinguished on the basis of food-non-food and old land-new land criteria. The relative food price is determined endogenously, and it influences the allocation of land between the food and non-food subsectors.

Experimental applications of the modified models are still under way by national researchers in the respective countries. What is important at this stage is the impossibility of adapting and/or estimating the fertility and mortality functions of the prototype model. Hence, exogenous demographic projections on different alternatives are being used in the simulation runs in both countries.

The Structural Components of the Economic-Demographic Models

A contribution in this Report by SANDERSON /1977/ reviews and critically examines five simulation models which have elements of economic-demographic interactions and also include specifically an agricultural sector. Besides the PT2 Model /MARTOS 1977/ discussed in more detail above since it forms an integral part of this Report, the other models are the Bachue-2 /Wéry et al. 1974/, the Tempo-II /McFarland et al. 1973/, the Simon /Simon 1976/ and the Kelley, Williamson and Cheetham Model-KWC /Kelley et al. 1972/.

The following discussion does not purport to repeat the Sanderson critique. It will instead highlight some of the themes pursued in this Report with respect to the role of agriculture in economic-demographic interactions, and it will suggest the extent to which these themes have come up in the modelling work reviewed. We hasten to add that we do not propose to judge these models by "an ideal standard". Each model was built for a specific reason, and the standard by which it should be judged is whether it does or does not do the job for which it was built - a theme which Sanderson covers adequately. Moreover, even the most successful operational model can always be "improved" by considering other relationships which make it more "realistic". The model-builder, nevertheless, has to tread carefully a thin line between constructing a model which is simple enough to be readily implementable and complex enough to be adequately realist. The purpose of our discussion, therefore, is to demonstrate how difficult it is to account fully for the economic-demographic interactions within an implementable modelling framework.

The Agricultural Economy Side of Economic-Demographic Models

On the economy side, modelling economic-demographic relations can travel a well-trodden path, since the agricultural production relationships have been well investigated in the literature, and there exist a number of functional forms from among which the modeller can choose.

The first question that arises is the degree of detail in which the agricultural sector is described. The specification merely of an agricultural sector, as is the case with the Tempo II model, the Simon model and the KWC model, can still produce some agriculture-specific economic-demographic interactions. It will be impossible, however, to deal with questions such as land reform, farm size, modernization of agriculture and other topics which are of specific interest to agricultural policy-makers. The Bachue-2 model distinguishes three subsectors within agriculture, domestic food crops, export crops and livestock-fishing-forestry. The PT2 model as adapted for application to Pakistan distinguishes four agricultural subsectors which were of special interest in the implementation for that country - small-scale farming in rainfed regions, small-scale farming in irrigated regions, large-scale farming in rainfed regions and large-scale farming in irrigated regions.

The second question is the specification of the production relationships in agriculture. Labour is considered a crucial factor of production in agriculture, with the exception of the prototype PT2 model in which agricultural production grows in response to investment in land expansion and investment in intensification and therefore it is assumed that labour is free. In addition to the realism of this assumption (even for large-scale farms?), the specification rules out, among others, treatment of the migration process within the agricultural sector as endogenous, or relating fertility behaviour to the costs and benefits of children within the mode of operation of the farm firm. The other extreme is represented by the Tempo II model in which agricultural output is produced by labour alone and the entire agricultural population is assumed to be working. No agricultural unemployment is allowed in the Bachue 2 model either, since the domestic food crops sub-sector and the livestock fishing-forestry subsector are assumed to employ the residual number of workers who are not employed elsewhere. The output of export agriculture in that model is assumed to be proportional to the labour input. A more sophisticated specification of the production process is through a Cobb-Douglas production function in capital, labour and infrastructure (Simon), or even better a constant-elasticity-of-substitution (CES) production function (KWC). These models also incorporate technological change — neutral for the former and non-neutral, embodied, for the latter.

The economic-demographic modelling of the development process must account, as a minimum, for the change in the size of the agricultural sector, in relation to non-agriculture. Ideally, it should also account for the change in the composition of the agricultural output. These features should become endogenous in the development process. This implies the use of prices which are determined by the interaction of supply and demand. This interaction feature is very rare. The Bachue 2 model, for example, is exclusively a demand-oriented model of development. Only the KWC model deals with the problem of endogenizing the sectoral composition of output by introducing a Stone-Geary system of demand equations. The general equilibrium model which results from the combination of the supply and the demand side in the KWC model simultaneously determines the relative price ratios, output levels, consumption, investment and the functional distribution of income. This feature is important for policy-making to the extent that an important policy instrument is changing the terms of trade between agriculture and non-agriculture. The impact of such policies on variables such as output, employment, utilization of other inputs such as fertilizer, the level of migration can only be investigated within such a model.

This short list of the crucial features of the agricultural economy side of economic-demographic modelling is certainly not exhaustive. The economy side is bound to involve other variables as well which will be endogenously determined, such as savings ratios, capital formation etc. The complete list of these variables, and the way in which they are handled, would depend on the characteristics of the particular economy one wishes to study.

The Demography Side of Economic-Demographic Modelling

The demography side of the economic-demographic models may include a demographic accounting system plus behavioural submodels which determine a set of endogenous demographic variables. Not all models reviewed are complete on the demography side, and our discussion will touch upon the range of alternatives utilized there.

A demographic accounting system is needed as a minimum to cover the age-sex-sectoral composition of the population and the educational structure of the population. The practice in this respect varies among the models reviewed. The KWC model, for example, entirely ignores the age structure of the population, while Bachue 2 is the most elaborate. It divides the population into 180 categories, 15 age groups, two sex groups, two location groups and three education groups. On the basis of these, the system can be built up from the base year by using vital statistics to follow the number of people who are one year older in year t+1, two years older in year t+2, etc. The PT2 model, on the other hand, uses grouped data for the demographic accounting system and therefore cannot age the population in a straightforward manner by applying single years of age survival rates.

The age-structure of the population is the basic ingredient for constructing the education accounting system, by matching population with school attendance ratios and reconstructing the age distribution of school leavers. Similarly, the labour force participation rate is derived by starting from the age-sex structure of the population. Both education and labour force participation, however, need to go beyond the demographic accounting system in order to integrate the demand and the supply side. At this point, specific submodels are needed to specify further the relationships and to follow up their interrelations with other aspects of the model, such as the production decisions or the fertility decisions. At this stage, in other words, the model builder must ask the question, for example, what determines how many of the children of age 18 to 22 attain university education, or what determines how many women of working age actually seek employment. Furthermore, the indirect impact of education on the production model and on the fertility decisions must be examined. The models reviewed are all weak on the behavioural aspects of education and labour force participation. In the PT2 model, for example, the impact of education is exclusively on fertility.

A crucial component of any economic-demographic modelling work is the fertility submodel. This starts from the demographic accounting system and the age-sex distribution of the population, and introduces behavioural considerations from the demography and economy side. The PT2 model, for example, makes the rate of change in fertility a function of education and of the change of job opportunities for women in the modern sector. The Bachue 2 model is more sophisticated, at least on the demography side. First it predicts the age-specific marriage rates by the use of a nuptiality function. The second step would be to use the age-of-marriage information in order to construct functions of age-specific marital fertility rates. The version of the Bachue 2 model reviewed here, however, stops short of that, and formulates, instead, a birth-rate function with arguments the life expectancy at birth, educational characteristics, the duration of family planning programmes and the labour force participation of women aged 15-44. This is, of course, a serious shortcoming of the model, since birth-rates are to a great extent determined by the age structure of the population, and can thus change simply as a result of the demographic history of a population. The appropriate behavioural variable for the analysis is the fertility rate.

The simplest way to treat mortality rates is to consider them exogenous and generate them from a model life table system, given a value of the life expectancy at birth (e.g. the PT2 model). The alternative is to consider mortality rates an endogenous variable, and to estimate them within a submodel. The Bachue 2 submodel for mortality (or rather life expectancy) has as arguments the level of income and its distribution.

Interactions between the Economy and the Demography Side

The models reviewed describe the process of development in terms of mechanisms originating on both the economy and the demography side.   These are mechanisms such as technological change, population growth, growth in the stock of human and physical capital, increased specialization associated with increased market size, and so on.   However, all the models are weak in capturing the interactions which go from economic development to demographic change.   No attempt is made, for example, to describe the mechanism by which intermediate developmental variables may influence fertility behaviour.   As a result, the question: what are the policy variables which operate on development and can be more effective in affecting fertility behaviour is at best mute.   On the other hand, interactions which go from demographic change to economic development are more thoroughly covered, since the population antecedents of development are more familiar in the literature.

The conclusion from this discussion is that there is need for more micro-economic research on the developmental determinants of fertility.   Only then will it become possible to formulate precise hypotheses linking demographic behaviour with the process of economic development.

CHAPTER VI

ON INTRODUCING ECONOMIC-DEMOGRAPHIC INTERACTIONS
IN AGRICULTURAL PLANNING

This chapter is concerned with the possible uses in planning, particularly for agriculture, of the insights gained from the discussion in the previous chapters and more generally from the general debate concerning population-development relationships. The corollary of this debate is that those responsible for promoting agricultural development would do a better job if they were to account in their work as far as possible for the influence that a changing demographic situation exerts on the prospects and requirements for the socio-economic development of the sector. Moreover the type and rate of socio-economic development occurring and/or promoted by planners in agriculture exerts influence on demographic change itself (e.g. fertility, migration). Therefore, if mounting demographic pressure (or a particular dimension of it, e.g. urban congestion, unemployment) is considered a "problem", appropriate planning of agriculture in the context of a national population policy would contribute to slowing it down (e.g. by pursuing fertility reductions through the promotion of appropriate socio-economic change) or otherwise influence it.

One task here will be to see to what extent these propositions can be translated into operational terms for influencing planning practices. In this context, it is useful to distinguish three relevant aspects of the population-development debate:

First, part of the debate and the relevant literature amounts to little more than further elaboration of the conventional treatment of demographic change in economics. This discipline has tended to view demographic change as representing variation in one factor of production (labour), in the number of consumers, and generally in the number of beneficiaries of development. This approach includes the aspects of the debate which refer to changes in factor proportions, in the mix of investment allocations, the analysis of employment, or analysis of consumption taking into account the age and sex structure of the population. The relevance of this part of the debate for planning is to be found mostly in the area of the methodology, i.e. how best to utilize demographic information so

as to improve demand analysis, employment analysis, and generally the analytical work
preceding the plan preparation.

Second, the extensive discussion of the feed-back relationships from the socio-economic
sphere to demography, and in particular the attempts to establish empirically such relationships, represent an aspect of the debate which has introduced some "novel" ideas into the
universe of the "conventional" economic planner. The extent to which this novelty has
influenced or can be expected to influence traditional economic planning remains uncertain,
and such influence is likely to be uneven between different aspects of demographic change.
For example, the idea and empirical evidence that socio-economic variables influence such
demographic variables as migration or labour force participation rates (LFPRs) can find
ready use in most planning work. However, the part of the debate relating socio-economic
change to fertility may prove much more difficult to utilize in a "conventional" planning
context.

Third, a good part of the population-development debate is devoted to the discussion
of ways and means (strategies, policies, courses of action, etc.) aimed at coping with
problems caused by, or related to, mounting population pressure, particularly in the
context of resource-poor countries and of the international economic order. The relevant
discussion is not unrelated to the trends in the more general development thinking in the
seventies during which there has been a shift away from almost exclusive preoccupation with
aggregate economic growth towards questions of equity and priority for the satisfaction of
the "basic needs" of the most underprivileged groups of the population /Todaro 1977/. The
factors that contribute to development have also been subjected to a reassessment which
has tended to give prominence to such "social" variables as forms of social organization
or ideology, at the expense of the central role assigned by more conventional thinking to
capital formation.

The significance for planning of this part of the population-development debate
should be sought primarily in its influence on the way in which planners conceive development processes and goals and the role of the public sector, and hence of themselves. To
the extent that it will induce planners to reexamine conventional (capital formation centred)
interpretations of development, it may be expected to eventually exert a profound influence

on planning practices. Attempts to translate the relevant concerns into actual planning practice have already started appearing in the literature under such names as Food and Nutrition Planning, Redistribution with Growth, or Planning for Basic Needs /Chenery et al. 1974, Pyatt and Thorbecke 1976, FAO 1975b/.

It is, however, beyond the scope of this report to review the state of the arts in this area, notwithstanding the considerable overlapping with the population-development debate. We shall attempt instead to address in more detail the question of (a) the extent to which agricultural planning could be improved through the utilization of demographic information and (b) the extent to which planned socio-economic change in agriculture could be made a factor in the pursuit of desired change in the demographic sector.

Accounting for Demographic Change in Plan Preparation

Projections of total population are normally a starting point in any plan preparation. In this sense, agricultural planners have always accounted for demographic change in their work. The contention that agricultural planning can be improved by incorporating demographic change should therefore be taken to imply that a more appropriate handling of the total population variable and, more important, accounting for additional dimensions of demographic change will result in better (more purposeful, more accurate) agricultural plans and policies.

In almost all cases of agricultural plan preparation, demographic change over the plan period is taken as exogenous. In such cases the question of concern here is the extent to which the planner can utilize fairly disaggregated demographic projections and the difference which this will make to the "quality" of the plan. Thus, in addition to global population projections, the planner may find it useful to incorporate additional dimensions of "exogenous" demographic change such as age and sex structure, labour force participation rates, distribution of population by region and urban-rural category, and, of course, the cross classification of these variables, i.e. population in each region by age and sex, rural/urban and active/non-active distinctions.

The use of such information will presumably depend, inter alia, on the kind of plan under preparation, the methods of analysis, and the kind of non-demographic information used. Let us take the most common case of the preparation of a five-year sector plan without the aid of a comprehensive sector planning model. In such cases, the process of plan preparation will most commonly involve the following broad phases:

(a) projections of total demand for food and other agricultural products for the terminal year, including an analysis of the nutritional implications of the projections (demand analysis);

(b) an analysis and evaluation of the potential of the different resources and other factors in agriculture to be increased, modified, or otherwise made more productive so that increases in production can be obtained (supply analysis);

(c) an evaluation of the role of the different policy instruments in bringing about the desired change as identified under (a) and (b), and the determination of the level and modalities of their use within the constraint of total resource availabilities for this purpose.

In the case of demand analysis, and if only a total population projection is used, the estimation of food requirements for the terminal year is obtained by multiplying total projected population by an average national per capita consumption level for that year. The latter can be a normative figure, or it can be estimated with the aid of the per capita income growth, demand functions and elasticities. The implied nutritional situation can only be evaluated in terms of national average indicators and the resulting analysis of welfare and policy issues is of very limited value.

By contrast, the use of disaggregated demographic information will make it possible to obtain more realistic and accurate estimates of food requirements for the terminal year (as well as to set nutritional objectives and evaluate implications), in the following ways:

(a) food needs and/or effective demand are influenced by the age and sex structure of the population. The most common way of accounting for this dimension of demographic change is by "homogenizing" the total population projection with the aid of different food consumption weights applied to the different sex and age groups;

(b) the distribution of population by region will make it possible to account for region-sepcific differentials in food consumption, e.g. differences in living standards (per capita incomes) affecting the level and structure of the diet; or differences in agro-climatic conditions influencing the volume and pattern of food production, thus determining the kind and quantity of food supplies which people have access to, and/or preference for, in each region;

(c) in rural areas food consumption patterns and levels are intricately linked to the predominant economic activity of the rural population—agriculture. The link is to be found mainly in the phenomenon of production for own consumption or, in particular societies, the use of food as a means of payment for agricultural labour, including the provision of some degree of year round minimum food security. By contrast, the urban population depends to a much greater extent on a system of monetary transactions. Factors affecting the income earning opportunities and the functioning of the trade and distribution system are, therefore, important determinants of food consumption levels in the urban areas. It may also be that food import opportunities play a key role in the food consumption standards of the urban people. Furthermore, the different occupational structures and life styles of the two population groups make for important differences in their food consumption behaviour. It is thus clear that the availability of disaggregated estimates of future population by rural and urban groups will help the planner to account for the particular characteristics of each group, and thus lead to more reliable estimates of future food requirements.

However, the availability of disaggregated demographic information per se will not greatly help the planner unless he also has access to appropriate information concerning the characteristics of the different population groups distinguished (incomes, behaviour patterns).

The above discussion has assumed that food demand is treated as a separate area of analysis in plan preparation. In the particular case of food demand analysis of the rural population, this separate treatment may substantially reduce the benefits. As already mentioned, decisions of the rural households concerning food consumption are intimately linked to decisions on production and resource use and conceivably also to decisions of a purely demographic character (family size, migration of family members). The benefits from better integration of demographic factors can therefore only be realized fully if food demand analysis is treated as an integral part of analysis concerning production and other aspects of agriculture.

As to the phase of supply analysis, we note that the projections of demand represent an important factor in guiding decisions and policies for influencing what to produce, how much, where and how.   To the extent that the different approaches to demand analysis under the two alternatives have resulted in significantly different estimates of volume, pattern and perhaps spatial distribution of demand, the decisions and policies for influencing the growth, structure and spatial distribution of production will therefore also be different.

With regard to the latter aspect, we noted in an earlier chapter how the variation in per capita calorie levels between States in India seems to be closely related to the interstate variation in foodgrains production rather than to differentials in incomes. This clearly indicates the need for production planning to be guided by information on the distribution of population between regions.   The experience of Kerala /PANIKAR et al. 1977/ is also instructive when planning for production increases under mounting demographic pressure and deteriorating land/man ratios.   In that State, when population increases exceeded the carrying capacity of lands suitable for rice cultivation, the farmers responded by introducing among other things inter- and mixed cropping of a variety of root crops (yams, colocasia) along with the main commercial crops.   This response is regarded by the authors as an important contribution to the maintenance of food supplies and as possibly having helped avert famine.

The availability of disaggregated and reliable estimates of the agricultural/rural labour force can also exert a profound influence on policy choices for promoting production increases.   Estimates of the labour force will be used as a necessary input into the process of selecting cropping patterns and technologies, since different crops and technologies have different labour-use requirements.   The level and mix of particular policy instruments such as investments or the provision of modern inputs will therefore be affected accordingly.   Moreover, labour represents an input into the production but also a resource which has to be employed to the fullest extent possible.   The relative abundance or scarcity of labour will thus influence the priorities attached to different development objectives, e.g. output maximization (implying "optimal" use of labour), employment promotion or income distribution.   The extent to which labour is employed is not simply a matter of cropping patterns and technologies, but also depends on agricultural asset ownership and control, the institutional organization and on social relations.   An increased awareness by the planners of population-related problems (made possible, by, inter aiia, the availability of disaggregated demographic information) can thus have far reaching implications on the role assigned to policy intervention in the sector.

In the discussion so far, we have referred to the most common cases of the handling of demographic variables exogenously when the analytical techniques used for agricultural plan preparation are of a fairly informal nature. The situation does not change signifi- cantly when formal models of the agricultural sector are used as planning aids. However, a formal model, being an explicit and fairly rigorous statement of the functioning of the sector /Alexandratos 1976/ provides an opportunity for observing in more concrete terms the use made of demographic variables.

Taking as an example the most common case of linear programming models with regional structures and endogenous prices, e.g. the one of the agricultural sector of Tunisia /Condos and Cappi 1976/, we can identify three demographic variables entering the calculus. These are the total population, the distribution of population by region (hence, internal migration) and the agricultural labour force.

The values of all three variables over the period of model application are taken as exogenous. Generally speaking, projections of the total and regional population are used to position in the price quantity coordinate space the demand schedules for products traded nationally or only regionally, respectively. Since the model simultaneously determines prices and quantities through the interaction of demand and supply, it follows that alternative values of total population and its regional distribution can have important effects on the solution concerning levels and patterns of production, consumption, incomes and resource use in the sector.

The agricultural labour force variable is further broken down by region, season, and institutional status (family or hired labour). The relevant projections are entered into the model as constraints. Parametric variation permits the evaluation of alternative policies for their impact on agricultural employment /Alexandratos et al. 1977/.

Alternative models of the agricultural sector used in development planning, particularly of the systems simulation type, may include a specific demographic submodel for producing the values of the demographic variables used in the other submodels of the system. However, the demographic submodel is driven by factors (e.g. rates of fertility, mortality, migration, labour force participation) which remain exogenous to developments in agriculture as portrayed in the sector model. The Korean agricultural sector model whioh belongs to this family has made a first timid effort to endogenise migration by allowing for the possibility of off-farm migration to be "... specified exogenously or determined endogenously as a function of the gap between the demand for non-agricultural labour and the labour supplied by the internal growth of the non-farm population" /Lee et al. 1976; p.9/. Even with this modifi-cation, however, migration is made dependent on developments in the non-agricultural sector, and it therefore remains essentially exogenous to change in agriculture, except very indirectly through the impact of agriculture on labour demand in the rest of the economy.

Accounting for Feedback Effects

We turn now to the question of the extent to which it is feasible and necessary to account in agricultural plan preparation for the feedback effects of socio-economic change on the demographic sector.

In the preceding section we discussed the possible use in planning of the agricultural/rural labour force estimates when they are given exogenously to the planning exercise. In real life, however, the determinants of the rural labour force (rural-urban migration and LFPRs) are themselves functions of opportunities for employment and of other socio-economic conditions in agriculture (relative, that is, to what happens in other sectors/regions). Such factors are not all, or even for the most part, agricultural but reflect conditions in all sectors of the economy in their rural and non-rural manifestations (e.g. education opportunities, employment, etc.). It follows that any attempt on the part of the agricul-tural planner to ensure consistency by endogenizing the values of such demographic variables requires analysis at the economy-wide level. In such an analysis, the agricultural sector can be represented by a few aggregates and be made to interact with other sectors and the demographic system. [1] The results of such an aggregate analysis "with economic-demographic interaction" can then be treated by the agricultural planner as "exogenous" when preparing the detailed agricultural plan. If this possibility does not exist, the agricultural

---

[1] This is one of the possible uses in agricultural planning of global models of economic-demographic interaction; see below.

planner can do little to account for the feedback effects of relative socio-economic change in agriculture to migration and the labour force.

The question that arises is whether ignoring feedback effects would really make an appreciable difference to the quality of the plan. This question takes us to the heart of the matter. The tentative answer is that it all depends on: (a) which are the demographic variables subject to the feedback influences, and (b) what is the kind of plan we are preparing — more concretely, what kind of decisions are going to be influenced by its existence.

The feedback effects from agricultural change on _fertility_ can probably be ignored with impunity within the context of a five-year sectoral plan. The justification is that it is not worth trying to introduce into agricultural plan preparation the sophistication required for capturing feedback effects on fertility unless we have sufficient empirical evidence of the relevant relationships. Such empirical evidence is generally lacking, the more so in the case of those agriculture specific variables (technology, crop mix, labour use, rural institutions) which enter the calculus of the agricultural planner. Moreover, the kind of socio-economic change postulated in a five-year agricultural plan is unlikely to lead to the quantum jump which would bring to threshold levels those socio-economic variables tentatively hypothesized as being correlated with fertility.

This is not to deny that the longer term horizon is made up of a succession of short term planning intervals. We only contend that, _ceteris paribus_, a longer term planning horizon may be more appropriate for endogenizing the fertility variables, since it provides more room for socio-economic change to occur and attain the levels which may be instrumental in producing a fertility decline. Since many of the variables that are hypothesized (with varying degrees of empirical support) as correlates of fertility are not strictly agricultural (education, health, women's participation in modern sector employment), it follows that agricultural planning with endogenous fertility would require not only that a longer term planning horizon be adopted, but also that it be done in the context of economy-wide planning exercises. These restrictions may be relaxed (and some degree of endogenous fertility determination into routine agricultural planning can therefore be introduced) if and when it is established empirically that fertility is significantly related to "routine" agricultural variables such as demand and production structures, technology, farm size, and organization of production.

In the discussion in the preceding chapters, it was noted that nutrition may be significantly correlated to fertility and mortality. In the general case, nutrition is a significant component of the set of socio-economic variables which collectively reflect development and are negatively related to fertility. However, nutrition is a variable which, in its own right, is an important determinant of the physiological dimensions of fertility and mortality. Its role in women's fertility capability and behaviour is a case in point. Moreover, its effects on infant mortality and through it on fertility (desired number of surviving children), is a factor commonly cited as a prime example of feedback effects from socio-economic change to fertility.

The above considerations perhaps justify a special effort on the part of agricultural planners to try to internalize in the planning calculus the impact of nutrition (an essentially agriculture determined variable) on fertility and mortality. In cases where nutrition is already at acceptable levels this may not be very important. However, in planning for areas or countries with precarious and inadequate nutritional levels, the impact of variation of such levels (as may occur within the plan period) on demography may be significant and should be accounted for as far as possible. Indeed, in such situations, agricultural planning may have as a major goal the increase of food supplies and the improvement of nutrition; it will therefore stand to gain significantly from the explicit consideration of two-way interdependence of the improvements pursued in the sector with demography.

Let us now look in the same spirit at interdependence between agricultural variables and the other two demographic variables of concern here, viz. migration and labour force participation rates (LFPRs). We have already mentioned that the use of disaggregated demographic information would enable the planner to analyse the development problems and to design policies more efficiently. We also noted above that the individual components into which the demographic sector is disaggregated are themselves subject to change, as a consequence of changes occurring and/or brought about by planning in agriculture. Here our concern is to see in what particular planning context it is necessary and feasible to attempt to account for this two-way interaction.

In the first place, we note that migration and LFPRs may be expected to be much more sensitive than fertility to changing socio-economic conditions over the medium term. Changes occurring over a five-year planning period could therefore have a significant impact on these two demographic variables. If planning is of such a nature that policy decisions are significantly affected by the spatial distribution of the population or by the agricultural labour availability, we stand to gain by attempting to internalize in the planning mechanism the relationships affecting these two variables. Consider, for example, the case of regional planning or that of planning for the nutritional improvement of particular groups. In such cases, the definition of planning objectives and the mix and level of policy instruments are closely related to the numbers of people having the particular demographic characteristics, i.e. location or dietary inadequacy. It is obvious that, in such cases, a two-way interaction process should be incorporated into the planning calculus lest the demographic situation for which we are planning will not materialize. That this is not an idle academic concern is shown by the not infrequent lack of success of transmigration schemes (the refusal of the potential migrants to take up the opportunity to settle in newly opened areas) or, in the opposite case, by the failure of policies to retain people in agriculture in particular regions. Insofar as factors which induce people to move are generally hypothesized to be the comparative socio-economic conditions in one sector/region versus another, it follows that the socio-economic variables of concern will not be all agricultural and also that what is important is their comparative (between sector/region) rather than their absolute values. The attempt to endogenize economic-demographic interactions will therefore have to be done, at least partly, in an intersectoral planning framework.

By contrast, when planning is of such a nature that the policy prescriptions are not materially dependent on the values of particular demographic variables, we may be satisfied with treating those variables as exogenous. In any case, "good" exogenous demographic projections will always contain some elements of the feedback effects from socio-economic change to migration and LFPRs. Such projections normally reflect past trends, and hence contain the implicit assumption that (a) socio-economic change will largely continue as in the past, and (b) the mechanism relating socio-economic change to demographic change in the past will be largely valid also for the future. Unless we plan for rates and patterns of socio-economic change radically different from the past, we may therefore be satisfied with the implicit degree of endogeneity present in the "exogenous" demographic projections.

Possible Uses of Global Models of Economic-Demographic Interaction

In the preceding section we examined the manner in which demographic variables are handled in agricultural sector models used as planning aids. We concluded that one cannot speak of economic-demographic interaction proper since these models introduce demographic variables into the planning calculus exogenously. This is so even in cases of systems models of the sector, in which models the demographic system is represented by a special submodel which, however, is no more than a generator of demographic data.

The absence of interaction in agricultural sector models should come as no surprise. The investigation of economic-demographic interaction requires that socio-economic change be considered simultaneously in more than one sector. Moreover, agricultural sector models are geared to handle agricultural variables in the detail required by policy analysis work at the level of the sector, e.g. crop mixes, choice of technology, credit, seasonality of employment, investment, prices and subsidies.

Sectoral model builders will therefore find it difficult to reconcile their routine tasks with concerns for economic-demographic interaction. Even a special effort on their part to extend the scope of agricultural sector models to cover interaction is not likely to prove fruitful. This is so because there is at best a scanty knowledge of interdependence between routine agricultural variables such as the ones mentioned above (and which are indispensable if a sectoral model is to be of use to planners) and demographic variables, especially fertility.

In these circumstances, the agricultural planner concerned with population-development relationships could possibly turn for help to the multisectoral models especially developed for this purpose. Some of these models were reviewed briefly in Chapter V above. Here we are concerned with their possible value to the agricultural planner. In this context, the following considerations may apply. The problem of accounting for one way relation-ships from population to development (i.e. the consequences side) in agricultural planning

can be largely resolved in the manner suggested in the preceding section. Resort to a
model of economic-demographic interaction is not therefore required in principle. However,
sectoral planning proper needs to be referred to some kind of economy-wide analytical framework. Issues such as the intersectoral terms of trade, the role of agriculture in balance
of payments policy, investment availabilities to the sector or comparative employment
requirements are essential inputs into agricultural policy making which can be obtained
only from economy-wide analyses.

The question should thus be redefined as follows. Should the agricultural planner
refer his sectoral work to an economy-wide model of the economic-demographic type or rather
to one not designed to handle economic-demographic interaction? Ceteris paribus, a model
of the former type should be preferred since the raison d'être of these models is that
they account for economic-demographic interaction - an important factor conditioning socio-
economic development. However, one should be extremely cautious in taking this answer
at face value. For one thing, many of the inputs into agricultural planning derived from
economy-wide analyses are predominantly the results of the internal working of the socio-
economic part of the model. For another, models not belonging to the economic-demographic
interaction family normally account for the consequences side of demographic change anyway.

It is therefore only when one is convinced that the feedback loops characterizing
such models are important determinants of the guidance provided by economy-wide analyses
to agricultural planning that recourse to models of economic-demographic interaction is
justified. It is obvious that this is a problem which cannot be resolved in abstract
terms. It may be that the economic part of any given model of economic-demographic
interaction is weak in comparison to other available economic models - a not infrequent
case /SANDERSON 1977/. In such cases the agricultural planner would probably opt for a
model of the latter type. One should also recognize that broad strategic decisions
directly or indirectly influencing agriculture are not necessarily the domain of the
agricultural planner, although he may play a role in them. Hence, the choice of the type
of model to be used for providing the economy-wide framework for agricultural planning
may not really belong to him.

The conclusion of the discussion so far is that as far as the consequences side of population-development realtionships is concerned, the value of economic-demographic models to the agricultural planner will depend predominantly on how "good" their economic part is compared to other available models of the economy. When, however, a national population policy is of top priority in development planning, models of economic-demographic interaction may serve a useful purpose in the coordination of sectoral policies towards the attainment of objectives in the demographic sector. A national population policy based on the promotion of development patterns propitious to influencing fertility and migration will require contributions from all sectors, including agriculture.

Generally speaking, economic-demographic models will be useful if they are able to simulate successfully the response of fertility and migration to alternative packages of policies, some of which will require implementation in the context of agricultural planning. For example, policy packages used in experiments with the Bachue model /Rodgers and Wéry 1977/ contain a number of policies belonging to this category, e.g. promotion of agricultural investment, exports, and more efficient marketing.

Naturally, the same package in which such policies appear will generally contain policies in other sectors, e.g. education, health, industry, infrastructure etc. Since such policies also refer to rural areas where agriculture predominates they will need to be integrated with agricultural policies proper. It is an abstraction from reality to talk about the effects of agricultural policies on demography outside the context of the rural community and independently of other policies affecting the rural sector. This is important, not only for the investigation of economic-demographic interaction but also for any kind of planning geared to the improvement of the welfare of the rural population. There is already a relative shift in planning practices away from agricultural planning towards rural development planning, though many problems are still unresolved, particularly of a methodological and institutional (pertaining to the government planning apparatus) nature.

Conclusions

Development planners are being increasingly urged to incorporate population factors into planning. This we have interpreted to mean that they should view the development problem as being closely related to, and evolving with, a changing demographic situation, and that they should design and implement development policies accordingly. What is more important, development policies should be so designed as to influence demographic trends in a desirable direction.

In this chapter, we have endeavoured to explore the possibility of making agricultural planning demography responsive. We have looked into the different tasks involved in agricultural plan preparation with a view to identifying the role of demographic factors in the analysis of development problems, the definition of planning goals and the formulation and evaluation of policies.

Our conclusion is that planners have always accounted for demographic change in plan preparation, though mostly in an exogenous manner. There is, however, considerable room for improvement in the area of exogenous handling of demographic change, particularly by the use of disaggregated information to analyse problems and evaluate policies. Returns on this kind of extra effort by planners are likely to vary between countries/regions depending on the initial conditions, i.e. the extent to which demographic change is closely related to developments in some key welfare indicators already in a precarious state, e.g. nutrition, employment, poverty.

More generally, preoccupation with considerations of equity and satisfaction of basic needs means that planning is increasingly concerned with, and directed at, specific groups of the population. The concept of "target group" defined as "a group of people who are not only all poor but also relatively homogeneous with respect to the effect that a given set of policy instruments might have on them" /Bell and Duloy 1974/ is being developed in response to planning needs. Demographic information on the size, structure and location of specific population groups as well as the dynamics of their change over time has thus come to be an indispensable input into policy formulation and evaluation.

As regards the possibility of making agricultural policies influence demographic developments (mostly fertility), our conclusion is that agricultural planners can best contribute to population policies in the context of multisectoral planning efforts, particularly for the rural population. This conclusion reflects, inter alia, the limitations of agricultural planning in this field because of the paucity of empirical knowledge concerning the extent to which agricultural variables handled in the course of

plan preparation are correlates of fertility.

REFERENCES*

Abercrombie, K.C. /1969/, "Population Growth and Agricultural Development," FAO Monthly Bulletin of Agricultural Economics and Statistics, Vol. 18, (April).

Adelman, I. /1963/, "An Econometric Analysis of Population Growth," American Economic Review, 53:3 (June), pp. 314-338.

Adelman, I. and C. Morris /1966/, "A Quantitative Study of Social and Political Determinants of Fertility," Economic Development and Cultural Change, (January), pp. 129-157.

Agency for International Development /1973/, United States Department of State, AID, Spring Review of Small Farmer Credit, Vols. 1-20, Washington.

Alexandratos, N. /1975/, "Handling of Demographic Variables in Agricultural Planning," Report on the FAO/UNFPA Seminar on Agricultural Planning and Population, Rome: FAO, pp. 52-61.

Alexandratos, N. /1976/, "Formal Techniques of Analysis for Agricultural Planning," FAO Monthly Bulletin of Agricultural Economics and Statistics, Vol. 25 (June) pp. 1-7.

Alexandratos, N., L. Naiken, and W. Schulte /1977/, "Demographic Variables in Sectorial Policies: The Case of Agricultural Development," paper presented to the International Union for the Scientific Study of the Population, Mexico (August).

ANDORKA, R. /1977/, "LONG-TERM DEMOGRAPHIC DEVELOPMENTS IN HUNGARY IN A HISTORICAL PERSPECTIVE," Rome: FAO (mimeo).

Anker, R. /1974/, An Analysis of International Variations in Birth Rates: Preliminary Results, Population and Employment Working Paper No. 3, Geneva: ILO.

Arghiri, E. /1972/, Unequal Exchange: A Study of Imperialism of Trade, New York: Monthly Review Press.

Arthur, W., and G. McNicoll /1975/, "Large-Scale Simulation Models in Population and Development: What Use to Planners?" Population and Development Review, Vol. 1 (December) pp.251-265.

Baldwin, K.D.S. /1975/, Demography for Agricultural Planners, Rome: FAO.

Barnum, H.W., and R.H. Sabot /1976/, Migration, Education and Urban Surplus Labour: The Case of Tanzania, Paris: Organization for Economic Cooperation and Development, Development Centre Studies, Employment Series No.13.

Bell, C. /1976/, "Fertility, Mortality and the Standard of Living," Washington: The World Bank (mimeo).

Bell, C. and J. Duloy /1974/, "Formulating a Strategy," Chapter VI in Chenery et al. (1974).

Berelson, B. /1976/, "Social Science Research on Population: A Review," Population and Development Review, Vol 2 (June), pp. 219-266.

* References in capital letters denote papers produced under the same project as this Report; see Appendix.

Birdsall, N. and R. Faruqee /1977/, "Population-Development Relationships: Approaches to Analysis," Washington: The World Bank, Population and Human Resources Division (mimeo).

Bliss, C., and N. Stern /1976/, "Economic Aspects of the Connection Between Productivity and Consumption, Part I: The Theory, Part II: Some Observations," University of Essex (mimeo).

BLISS, C. AND N. STERN /1977/, "PRODUCTIVITY, WAGES AND NUTRITION IN THE CONTEXT OF LESS DEVELOPED COUNTRIES," Rome: FAO (mimeo).

Boserup, E. /1974/, "Employment of Women in Developed Countries," in L. Tabah (ed.), Population Growth and Economic Development in the Third World. Belgium: Ondine Edition for the International Union for the Scientific Study of Population, pp. 79-107.

Boserup, E. /1975/, The Conditions of Agricultural Growth. Chicago: Aldine.

Boulding, E. /1976/, "Comments" in Douglas W. Toss (ed.), The Challenge of Overpopulation and Food Shortages (Summary of a Colloquium held in cooperation with Planned Parenthood Association of Northeast Texas and the Population Crisis Committee). New York: The Conference Board Inc., pp. 53-55.

Boyer, P., and A. Richard /1975/, "Elements d'Analyse de la Transition Demographique," Population (Paris) No. 4-5 (October), pp. 825-847.

Brown, L.R. /1970/, Seeds of Change. New York: Praeger.

Cain, G.G., and A. Weininger /1973/, "Economic Determinants of Fertility: Results from Cross-sectional Aggregate Data," Demography, Vol. 10, No. 12 (May), pp. 205-223.

Cairncross, J. /1977/, An Approach to Food/Population Planning. Rome: FAO.

Caldwell, J.C. /1976/, "Toward a Restatement of Demographic Transition Theory," Population and Development Review, Vol. 2 (September-December), pp. 321-356.

Calloway, D., and H. Spector /1954/, American Journal of Clinical Nutrition, 2, p. 405.

Chavez, A., and C. Martinez /1973/, "Nutrition and Development of Infants from Poor Areas. III. Maternal Nutrition and its Consequences on Fertility," Nutrition Reports International, Vol. 7, pp. 1-8.

Chayanov, A.V. /1925/, Theory of the Peasant Economy. Edited by D. Thorner, B. Kerblay and R.Z.F. Smith for the American Economic Association Service, Homewood, Illinois: Richard Irwin, 1966.

Chenery, H. M. Ahluwalia, C. Bell, J. Duloy, and R. Jolly /1974/, Redistribution with Growth, London: Oxford University Press.

Chenery, H., and J. Syrquin /1975/, Patterns of Development 1950-1970. London: Oxford University Press.

Clark, C. /1967/, Population Growth and Land Use. New York: St. Martin's Press.

Coale, A., and E. Hoover /1958/, Population Growth and Economic Development in Low Income Countries. Princeton: Princeton University Press.

Condos, A., and C. Cappi /1976/, "Agricultural Sector Analysis: A Linear Programming Model for Tunisia," FAO, (mimeo).

Dantwala, M.L. /1966/, "Institutional Credit in Subsistence Agriculture" International
    Journal of Agrarian Affairs, Vol. 5 No. 1, (December), pp. 52-61.

De Castro, J. /1952/, The Geography of Hunger. Boston: Little Brown.

Davidson, S., R. Passmore, J.F. Brock and A.S. Truswell /1975/, Human Nutrition and
    Dietetics, 6th edition. Edinburgh: Churchill Livingston.

Dell'Amore, G. /1973/, Agricultural Credit Markets of Africa (a series of monographs
    under the general editorship of Professor Giordano Dell'Amore) Milan: Cassa
    di Risparmio Delle Provincie Lombarde.

Drakatos, C.G. /1969/, "The Determinants of Birth Rate in Developing Countries, An
    Econometric Study of Greece," Economic Development and Cultural Change,
    Vol. 17, No. 4 (July), pp. 596-603.

Durand, J.D. /1974/, "The Labour Force in Economic Development and Demographic
    Transition," in Tabah, Leon (ed.), Population Growth and Economic Development
    in the Third World. Belgium: Ondine Edition for the International Union for
    the Scientific Study of Population.

Durnin, J. and R. Passmore /1967/, Energy, Work and Leisure. London: Heineman.

Ekanem, I., /1972/, "A Further Note on the Relation Between Economic Development and
    Fertility," Demography (Washington), Vol. 9, No. 3 (August), pp. 383-398.

El-Issawy, I. and A. El-Shafei /1977/, A Multi-Sectoral Economic-Demographic Simulation
    Model of the Egyptian Economy, Cairo: Institute of National Planning (mimeo).

Encarnación, J. Jr. /1974/, Fertility and Labour Force Participation: Philippines 1968,
    Population and Employment Working Paper No. 2, Geneva: ILO.

Epstein, T.S. /1962/, Economic Development and Social Change in South India. Manchester:
    Manchester University Press.

FAO /1975a/, Report on the FAO/UNFPA Seminar on Methodology, Research and Country Case
    Studies on Population, Employment and Productivity, Rome: FAO.

FAO /1975b/, Food and Nutrition Planning, Nutrition Consultants Reports Series No. 35,
    Rome: FAO.

FAO /1976/, "A Systems Simulation Approach to Integrated Population and Economic Planning
    with Special Emphasis on Agricultural Development and Employment: An Experimental
    Study of Pakistan" Rome (mimeo draft).

FAO/WHO /1973/, Energy and Protein Requirements, Report of a joint FAO/WHO Ad hoc
    Expert Committee, Rome: FAO.

Farooq, G. and B. Tuncer /1974/, "Fertility and Economic and Social Development in Turkey -
    A Cross-sectional and Time Series Study," Population Studies. (London) Vol. 28,
    No. 2 (July), pp. 263-276.

Freedman, D. /1963/, "The Relation of Economic Status to Fertility," The American Economic
    Review, No. 53 (June), pp. 414-426.

Garrow, J.S. /1974/, Energy Balance and Obesity in Man. Holland: Elsevier.

Gopalan, C. and K. Vijaya Raghavan /1969/, Nutrition Atlas of India. Hyderabad: National
    Institute of Nutrition, Indian Council of Medical Research.

Guest, A.M. /1973/, "The Relationship of the Crude Birth Rate and its Components to Social and Economic Development," Demography (Washington), Vol. 11, No. 3 (August), pp. 457-472.

Hansen, A.H. /1939/, "Economic Progress and Declining Population Growth," American Economic Review, 29 (March), pp. 1-15.

Haswell, M. /1975/, The Nature of Poverty. London: MacMillan.

Hayami, Y. and V. Ruttan /1971/, Agricultural Development: An International Perspective. Baltimore: Johns Hopkins University Press.

Heer, D. /1966/, "Economic Development and Fertility," Demography (Washington), Vol. 3, No. 2 pp. 423-444.

Hicks, W.W. /1974/, "Economic Development and Fertility Change in Mexico 1950-1970," Demography (Washington), Vol. 11, No. 3 (August), pp. 407-421.

Hirshman, A.O. /1958/, The Strategy of Economic Development. New Haven: Yale University Press.

Huenemann, R. /1975/, "Nutrition and Family Planning," Geneva: United Nations, World Health Organization (mimeo).

ILO /1975/, Growth, Employment and Equity: A Comprehensive Strategy for Sudan Vol. II Technical papers. Geneva.

ILO /1976/, International Recommendations on Labour Statistics. Geneva.

Inada, K. /1971/, "Development in Mono-cultural Economies," International Economic Review, 12, 2 (June), pp. 161-185.

Janowitz, B.S. /1973/, "An Econometric Analysis of Trends in Fertility Rates," Journal of Development Studies, (April), pp. 413-425.

Johnston, B.F. and P. Kilby /1975/, Agriculture and Structural Transformation. New York: Oxford University Press.

Jones, G.T. /1972/, "Basic Concepts and Definitions for Measurement of Under-utilization of Labour in Developing Countries, with Special Reference to Data Required for Rural Employment Policy." Rome: FAO (Document ESC/Misc 2, mimeo).

Jorgenson, D.W. /1969/, "The Role of Agriculture in Economic Development: Classical versus Neo-classical Models of Growth," in Wharton, C.R. (ed.) Subsistence Agriculture and Economic Development. Chicago: Aldine Publishing Co., pp. 320-348.

Kasarda, J.D. /1971/, "Economic Structure and Fertility: A Comparative Analysis," Demography 8:3, pp. 307-317.

Kelley, A.C., J.G. Williamson, and R. Cheetham /1972/, Dualistic Economic Development Chicago: University of Chicago Press.

King, T. (ed.) /1974/, Population Policies and Economic Development. Baltimore: Johns Hopkins University Press.

Kirk, D. and K.S. Srikanta /1969/, "Correlations of Natality in Countries of the Latin American Region," Food Research Institute, Stanford University (mimeo).

Kleinman, D.S. /1973/, "Fertility Variation and Resources in Rural India," Economic Development and Cultural Change, Vol. 21, No. 4 Part 1 (July), pp. 679-696.

Kocher, J.E. /1973/, Rural Development, Income Distribution and Fertility Decline. New York: The Population Council.

Krishna, R. /1973/, "Unemployment in India," Indian Journal of Agricultural Economics, Vol. 28 (January), pp. 1-23.

Lee Jeung Han, Kim Dong Min, and M. Abkin /1976/, "Structure and Application of the Korean Agricultural Sector Model" paper presented to the Regional Seminar on Agricultural Sector Analysis, Singapore: Agricultural Development Council, Inc. (November).

Leff, N. /1969/, "Dependency Rates and Savings Rates," American Economic Review (December).

Leibenstein, H. /1954/, A Theory of Economic-Demographic Development. Princeton: Princeton University Press.

Leibenstein, H. /1957/, "The Theory of Underemployment in Backward Economies," Journal of Political Economy, Vol. LXV, No. 2 (April), pp. 91-103.

Lewis, W.A. /1954/, "Economic Development with Unlimited Supplies of Labour," The Manchester School, 22 (May), pp. 139-191.

Lewis, W.A. /1958/, "Unlimited Supplies of Labour: Further Notes," The Manchester School, 26 (January), pp. 1-32.

Lluch, C. /1976/, "Theory of Development in Dual Economics: A Survey," The World Bank (mimeo).

LLUCH, C., AND J. BRUINSMA /1977/, "DEVELOPMENT IN DUAL ECONOMIES," Rome: FAO (mimeo).

MARTOS, B. /1977/, "SYSTEMS SIMULATION STUDIES FOR LONG-TERM POPULATION AND ECONOMIC PLANNING," Rome: FAO (mimeo).

McFarland, W.E. /1973/, "Description of the Tempo II Budget Allocation and Human Resources Model," General Electric-Tempo Working Paper GE73TMP-13.

McGreevey, W.P. and N. Birdsall /1974/, The Policy Relevance of Recent Research on Fertility. Washington, D.C: The Smithsonian Institution.

McKinnon, R. /1973/, Money and Capital and Economic Development. Washington: Brookings Institution.

McNamara, R.S. /1977/, "An Address on the Population Problem." Lecture delivered at the Massachusetts Institute of Technology, Cambridge, Mass. (April 28).

McNaughton, J. /1975/, "Population and Nutrition." Paper presented in the Seminar on Population and Food and Agricultural Development, Rome: FAO (December) (mimeo).

Meadows, D.H., D.L. Meadows, J. Randers, and W. Behrens III /1972/, The Limits to Growth, A Report for the Club of Rome's Project on the Predicament of Mankind. London: Earth Island.

Meadows, D. and J. Robinson /1977/, The Electronic Oracle, (forthcoming book manuscript).

Mountcastle, V.B. (ed.) /1968/, Medical Physiology. St. Louis: The C.V. Mosby Company.

Mueller, E. /1974/, "The Impact of Agricultural Change on Demographic Development in the Third World," in L. Tabah (ed.), Population Growth and Economic Development in the Third World. Belgium: Ondine Edition for the International Union for the Scientific Study of Population.

Mueller, E. /1976/, "The Economic Value of Children in Peasant Agriculture Households," in Ronald G. Ridker (ed.), Population and Development: The Search for Selective Interventions. Baltimore, The Johns Hopkins University Press, pp. 98-153.

Mundlak, Y. /1977/, "Agricultural Growth in the Context of Economic Growth." Paper presented to the 5th World Congress of the International Economic Association, Tokyo, (August).

Myrdal, G. /1968/, The Asian Drama. New York: Pantheon.

NAIKEN, L. /1977/, "DEMOGRAPHIC VARIABLES IN RELATION TO PLANNING FOR AGRICULTURAL DEVELOPMENT," Rome: FAO (mimeo).

Naiken, L. and W. Schulte /1976/, "Population and Labour Force Projections for Agricultural Planning," Food Policy, (May), pp. 192-202.

Nelson, R. /1956/, "A Theory of the Low-level Equilibrium Trap in Underdeveloped Economies," American Economic Review (December), pp. 894-908.

Oechsli, F. and Kirk /1975/, "Modernization and the Demographic Transition in Latin America and the Caribbean," Economic Development and Cultural Change, Vol. 23, No. 3 (April).

Ohlin, G. /1976/, "Economic Theory Confronts Population Growth," In Ansley Coale (ed.), Economic Factors in Population Growth. New York: John Wiley & Sons.

Oweis Jiryis, S. /1972/, Agricultural Policy in Developing Countries. Washington: U.S. Agency for International Development, Bureau for Programme and Policy Coordination, Office of Policy Development and Analysis.

Pandey, H.K. /1972/, "A Study of Credit Requirements and Advances to Farmers by Lead Bank in Varanasi, U.P." Economic Affairs, Vol. 17 Nos. 9-10, (September-October), pp. 442-447.

PANIKAR, P., T. KRISHNAN AND N. KRISHNAJI /1977/, "POPULATION GROWTH AND AGRICULTURAL DEVELOPMENT: A CASE STUDY OF KERALA," Trivandrum: Centre for Development Studies, and Rome: FAO (mimeo).

Pawley, W.H. /1971/, "In the Year 2070," Ceres: FAO Review, Vol. 4 (July) pp. 22-27.

Payne, P.R., and A.E. Dugdale /1975/, "A Stochastic Model for Energy Balance and Homeostasis," Department of Human Nutrition, London School of Hygiene and Tropical Medicine (mimeo).

Pepelasis, A., and P.A. Yotopoulos /1962/, Surplus Labour in Greek Agriculture, 1953-1960. Athens: Centre of Planning and Economic Research.

Population Reference Bureau, Inc. /1975/, "Literacy and World Population," Population Bulletin, Vol. 30, No. 2.

Pyatt, G., and E. Thorbecke /1976/, Planning Techniques for a Better Future, Geneva: ILO.

Quinn, J. /1977/, The Usefulness of Large-Scale Planning Models for Developing Countries, Bureau of the Census, U.S. Department of Commerce, (mimeo).

Ranis, G., and J.C.H. Fei /1961/, "A Theory of Economic Development," American Economic Review, 51 (September), pp. 533-565.

RTI, Research Triangle Institute /1971/, "Social and Economic Correlates of Family Fertility: A Survey of the Evidence" (September).

Reserve Bank of India /1969/, Report of All-India Rural Credit Review Committee. Bombay.

Rich, W. /1973/, Smaller Families Through Social and Economic Progress. Washington: Overseas Development Council.

Revelle, R. /1974/, "Food and Population," Scientific American, Vol. 231 (September), pp. 160-170.

Revelle, R. /1975/, "Will the Earth's Land and Water Resources be Sufficient for Future Population?" in United Nations, The Population Debate: Dimensions and Perspectives. New York: United Nations, Vol. 2.

Rodgers, G., and R. Wéry /1977/, The Effects of Economic Policy on Fertility, Population and Employment Working Paper No. 53, Geneva: ILO (mimeo).

SANDERSON, W. /1977/, "ECONOMIC-DEMOGRAPHIC SIMULATION MODELS: A REVIEW OF THEIR USEFULNESS FOR POLICY ANALYSIS," Rome: FAO (mimeo).

Sato, R. and Y. Niho /1971/, "Population Growth and the Development of a Dual Economy," Oxford Economic Papers, 23, 3 (November) pp. 418-436.

Schuh, E.D. /1976/, "Out-migration, Rural Productivity and the Distribution of Income" Washington: International Bank for Reconstruction and Development, Development Economics Department, Research Workshop on Rural-Urban Labour Market Interactions, (February).

Schulte, W., L. Naiken, and A. Bruni /1972/, "Projections of World Agricultural Population," FAO Monthly Bulletin of Agricultural Economics and Statistics, Vol. 21, No. 1 (January).

Schultz, T.P. /1971/, "Evaluation of Population Policies," Rand Corporation R-653-AID, Santa Monica, California.

Seers, D. /1973/, "The Meaning of Development," in C.K. Wilber (ed.) The Political Economy of Development and Underdevelopment. New York: Random House, pp. 6-14.

Simon, J.L. /1976/, "Population Growth May be Good for LDCs in the Long Run: A Richer Simulation Model," Economic Development and Cultural Change, Vo. 24, No.2, pp. 309-337.

Singh, J.N. /1974/, "Demographic Aspects of Employment in the Third World," in L. Tabah (ed.), Population Growth and Economic Development in the Third World. Belgium: Ondine Editions for the International Union for the Scientific Study of Population, pp. 707-740.

Snyder, D.W. /1974/, "Economic Determinants of Family Size in West Africa," Demography, (Washington) Vol. 11, No. 4, (November), pp. 613-627.

STARK, O. /1977/, "ECONOMIC-DEMOGRAPHIC INTERACTIONS IN THE PROCESS OF AGRICULTURAL DEVELOPMENT: THE CASE OF RURAL-TO-URBAN MIGRATION, SELECTED ISSUES AND SOME EVIDENCE," Rome: FAO (mimeo).

Taylor, C.E., /1973/, "Nutrition and Population," in A. Berg, N.S. Scrimshaw and David Call (eds.), Nutrition, National Development and Planning. Cambridge, Massachusetts: MIT Press, pp. 74-79.

Todaro, M. /1969/, "A Model of Labour Migration and Urban Unemployment in Less Developed Countries," American Economic Review, 59 (March), pp. 138-148.

Todaro, M. /1977/, "Development Policy and Population Growth: A Framework for Planners" Population and Development Review, Vol. 3 (March and June), pp. 23-43.

Turnham, D. /1971/, The Employment Problem in Less-Developed Countries: A Review of Evidence, Paris: OECD, Development Centre.

United Nations /1975/, Department of Economic and Social Affairs, Poverty, Unemployment and Development Policy: A Case Study of Selected Issues with Reference to Kerala. New York: United Nations (prepared by the Centre for Development Studies, Trivandrum) (ST/ESA/29).

United Nations /1977/, "Measuring the Impact of Socio-Economic Factors on Fertility in the Context of Declining Fertility: Problems and Issues," New York: United Nations, Department of Economic and Social Affairs, Population Division (Paper presented at the UN/UNFPA Expert Group Meeting on Demographic Transition and Socio-Economic Development, Istambul, 27 April-4 May 1977).

Vasthoff, J. /1968/, "Small Farm Credit and Development: Some Experience in East Africa with Special Reference to Kenya," Munich: IFO - Institut für Wirtschaftsforschung, Africa Studien 33.

Weintraub, R. /1962/, "The Birth Rate and Economic Development: An Empirical Study," Econometrica, XL, No. 4 (October) pp. 812-817.

Wéry R., G.C. Rodgers, and M.D. Hopkins /1974/, Bachue 2: Version I, A Population and Employment Model for the Philippines, Population and Employment Working Paper No. 5, Geneva: ILO.

Wishik, S.M., and S. Van der Vynckt /1975/, "Nutrition, Mother's Health and Fertility," in United Nations, The Population Debate: Dimensions and Perspectives. New York, pp. 605-612.

Wray, J.D., and A. Aguirre /1969/, "Protein-Calorie Malnutrition in Candelaria, Colombia, 1. Prevalence, Social and Demographic Causal Factors," Journal of Tropical Paediatry, 15, pp. 76-98.

Wray, J.D. /1972/, "Will Better Nutrition Decrease Fertility?" Paper presented at the Ninth International Nutrition Congress, Mexico City.

Yotopoulos, P.A. /1965/, "The Wage-Productivity Theory of Underemployment: A Refinement," The Review of Economics and Statistics, Vol. 32, No. (January).

Yotopoulos, P.A. and J.B. Nugent /1976/, Economics of Development: Empirical Investigations. New York: Harper and Row.

YOTOPOULOS, P.A. /1977/, "THE POPULATION PROBLEM AND THE DEVELOPMENT SOLUTION: INTERACTIONS ESPECIALLY IN AGRICULTURE," Rome: FAO (mimeo).

Zarembka, P. /1970/, "Marketable Surplus and Growth in the Dual Economy," Journal of Economic Theory, 2, 2 (June), pp. 107-121.

APPENDIX

OUTLINES OF PAPERS PREPARED UNDER THE
FAO/UNFPA PROJECT INT/73/P02*

---

* At the time of going to press (December 1977) these papers are available in final draft
form.   They will be produced in the course of the first half of 1978 and can be
requested from the Development Policy Studies and Training Service, Policy Analysis
Division, FAO, Rome.

Paper No. 1

<u>Title</u>

Long-Term Demographic Developments
in Hungary in a Historical Perspective

<u>Author</u>

Rudolf Andorka

Central Statistical Office, Budapest, Hungary

<u>Outline</u>

1. The Research Problem

2. Sources of Data

3. The Historical Periods Covered

4. The Pre-Industrial and Late Feudal Period (1700-1867)

    4.1 Population
    4.2 National Income and Agricultural Production
    4.3 Structure of the Economy
    4.4 Urban and Rural Population
    4.5 Social Structure of Hungarian Society and of Village Population
    4.6 Demographic Processes
    4.7 Case Studies Based on Family Reconstitution
    4.8 Summary

5. The Period of Industrial Take-off and of the Developing Capitalist Society (1867-1919)

    5.1 Population
    5.2 National Income and Agricultural Production
    5.3 Structure of the Economy
    5.4 Urban and Rural Population
    5.5 Social and Agrarian Structure
    5.6 Education
    5.7 Demographic Processes
    5.8 Fertility and Mortality Differentials
    5.9 Summary

6. The Period of Stagnating Capitalist Economy and Society (1920-1944)

    6.1 Population
    6.2 National Income and Agricultural Production
    6.3 Structure of the Economy
    6.4 Urban and Rural Population
    6.5 Social Structure of Hungary and of the Village Population
    6.6 Agrarian Structure
    6.7 Education
    6.8 Fertility, Mortality and Nuptiality
    6.9 Fertility and Mortality Differentials

Length

120 pages approximately

Paper No. 2

Title

The Population Problem and the Development Solution:
Interactions, Especially in Agriculture

Author

Pan A. Yotopoulos

Stanford University

Outline

Length

125 pages approximately

Paper No. 3

<u>Title</u>

Systems Simulation Studies for Long-Term
Population and Economic Planning ·

<u>Author</u>

Béla Martos

Institute of Economics, Hungarian Academy of Sciences, Budapest

Assisted by

Wuu-Long Lin, FAO, Rome

<u>Outline</u>

1. Premises

    1.1 Institutional Setting
    1.2 Long-term Planning
    1.3 Scope and Depth
    1.4 Methodology: Systems Simulation
    1.5 The Policy Concept

2. The Prototype Model PT2

    2.1 A Bird's-Eye View
    2.2 Sectoral Classification-Dualism
    2.3 National Accounts
    2.4 Agriculture and Food
    2.5 Labour Market
    2.6 Population and Related Socio-Economic Components
    2.7 Dynamics: Time Lags
          Appendix: Formalization of PT2

3. A Country Variant (Pakistan)
    3.1 Policy Issues. Data Availability
    3.2 Model Structure

4. Validity Tests
    4.1 Simulation at Work
    4.2 Testing PT1 (Data on Egypt)
    4.3 Testing PAK1 (Pakistan)
    4.4 The Moral of Validity Tests

<u>Length</u>

70 pages approximately

Paper No. 4

<u>Title</u>

Economic-Demographic Simulation Models:
A Review of their Usefulness for Policy Analysis

<u>Author</u>

Warren C. Sanderson

Stanford University

<u>Outline</u>

1. Introduction

2. Summary

3. The Bachue-2 Model

    3.1 Production Relations
    3.2 The Distribution of Income
    3.3 Savings
    3.4 The Components of Final Demand
    3.5 The Demographic Component
        3.5.1 The Demographic Accounting Equations
        3.5.2 Labour Force Participation Rates
        3.5.3 Education
        3.5.4 The Determinants of Fertility
        3.5.5 The Determinants of Mortality Rates
    3.6 Dynamic Aspects of the Bachue-2 Model
    3.7 The Treatment of Policy Questions

4. The Tempo II Model

    4.1 The Production Relations
    4.2 The Distribution of Income
    4.3 Savings
    4.4 The Determinants of Final Demand
    4.5 General Equilibrium Aspects
    4.6 The Demographic Component
        4.6.1 The Demographic Accounting
        4.6.2 Labour Force Participation Rates
        4.6.3 Education
        4.6.4 Fertility and Family Planning
        4.6.5 Nuptiality Rates
    4.7 Dynamic Considerations
    4.8 Policy Questions

5. The Simon Model

    5.1 Production Relations
    5.2 Social Indifference Curves and the Determination of Aggregate
        and Sectoral Output Levels
    5.3 Investment
    5.4 Technological Change
    5.5 The Demographic Component
    5.6 Conclusions

6. The FAO Model (adaptation of PT2 Model to Pakistan)
    6.1 Agriculture
    6.2 Industry
    6.3 Final Demand
    6.4 Employment
    6.5 Labour Force
    6.6 The Demographic Component
    6.7 Conclusions

7. The Kelley, Williamson and Cheetham Model
    7.1 The Relationships between Inputs and Outputs
    7.2 The Distribution of Income, Savings and Consumption
    7.3 General Equilibrium Considerations
    7.4 Dynamic Aspects
    7.5 Conclusions

Length

95 pages approximately

Paper No. 5

Title

Population Growth and Agricultural Development
A Case Study of Kerala

Authors

P.G.K. Panikar, T.N. Krishnan and N. Krishne

Centre for Development Studies, Trivandrum, I

Outline

1. Demographic Trends and their Implications – An Introduction

    1.1 Demographic Trends
    1.2 Impact of a High Rate of Population Growth

2. Agricultural Development with Unrestricted Imports of Food

    2.1 Introduction
    2.2 Exports and Agricultural Development
    2.3 Food Gap and Imports
    2.4 The Rationale of the Option

3. Changes in Cropping Pattern: Response to Uncertain Supplies from Outside

    3.1 Introduction
    3.2 Land Reclamation
    3.3 Trends in Cropping Intensity and Crop Pattern

4. Changes in the Distribution of Land: Demographic and Non-Demographic Factors

    4.1 The Distribution of Land
    4.2 Commercial Farming
    4.3 The Growth of Rural Wage Labour

5. Fertility Decline and Family Limitation

    5.1 Trends in Birth Rate of Kerala
    5.2 Trends in Age-specific Fertility Rates
    5.3 Changes in Nuptiality
    5.4 Changes in Marital Fertility
    5.5 Inter-Relationships between Education, Health and Decline in Fertility
    5.6 Conclusions

6. Internal and External Migration of the Population of Kerala: Causes and Consequences

    6.1 Nature and Extent of Out-migration from Kerala
    6.2 Internal Migration and Land Development
    6.3 Migration and Fertility
    6.4 Migration and Income Flow
    6.5 Conclusions

7. Summary and Conclusions

Length

90 pages approximately

- -

Paper No. 6

Title

Economic-Demographic Interaction in the Process of Agricultural Development:
The Case of Rural-to-Urban Migration - Selected Issues and Some Evidence

Author

Oded Stark

Bar-Ilan University, Ramat-Gan, Israel

Outline

1. Introduction

2. Utility, Technological Change, Surplus and Risk: An Outline of a New
Analytical Construct for Studying and Evaluating Rural-to-Urban Migration

3. Some Evidence

    3.1 Rural-to-Urban Migration as a Catalyst of Technological Change
         in Agricultural Production
    3.2 The Flow of Remittances
    3.3 Urban Unemployment of Rural-to-Urban Migrants
    3.4 Further Related Evidence Bearing on the Analytical Construct

4. The Impact of Rural-to-Urban Migration on the Distribution of Income by Size

5. Rural-to-Urban Migration and Fertility Decisions

6. Rural-to-Urban Migration, Social Welfare Criteria and Policy Oriented
   Implications: The Logical Inference of the Analytical Construct

<u>Length</u>

120 pages approximately

- -

Paper No. 7

<u>Title</u>

Productivity, Wages and Nutrition in the
Context of Less Developed Countries

<u>Authors</u>

Christopher Bliss, Nuffield College, University of Oxford

and

Nicholas Stern, University of Warwick

<u>Outline</u>

1. Introduction

2. The Theory

    2.1 The Positive Theory of Wages
    2.2 The Worker's Choice
    2.3 The Shadow Wage Rate and Employment Subsidies
    2.4 Choice of Family Size

3. Empirical Studies on Nutrition, Productivity, and Income

    3.1 Estimates of Number in Poverty
    3.2 Energy and Work
    3.3 Some Empirical Observations on Wages and Incomes

4. Suggestions for Further Work

<u>Length</u>

40 pages approximately

Paper No. 8

Title

Development in Dual Economies

Authors

Constantino Lluch

Development Research Centre, World Bank, Washington

and

Jelle Bruinsma, FAO, Rome

Outline

1. Introduction

2. Theories of Development in Dual Economies

3. The Segmented Economy Model

4. Numerical Analysis with the Segmented Economy Model

    4.1 Basic Development Processes
    4.2 Function Specification and Parameter Estimation
    4.3 The Standard Path
    4.4 Comparative Dynamics

5. Final Remarks

Length

20 pages approximately

- -

Paper No. 9

Title

Demographic Variables in Relation to Planning for Agricultural Development

Author

L. Naiken, FAO, Rome

Outline

1. Introduction

2. The Demographic Variables: Basic Concepts and Definitions

3. Approaches to Incorporation of Demographic Variables in Agricultural Planning Studies

4. Uses of Demographic Variables in FAO Country Perspective Studies

5. Alternative Population Growth Assumptions in the Country Perspective Studies

6. Conclusions

<u>Length</u>

19 pages approximately

4 721 G